This Is Poetry

Volume 3:
Poets of the West

Citizens for Decent Literature Press
a project of The Literary Underground

© Citizens for Decent Literature Press 2017

This Is Poetry
Volume III: Poets of the West

Editor:
Michele McDannold

Cover Art:
Michele McDannold

ISBN-10: 0692944818
ISBN-13: 978-0692944813

also available from Citizens for Decent Literature Press:
This Is Poetry Volume I: Women of the Small Press
This Is Poetry Volume II: The Midwest Poets

a project of The Literary Underground
theliteraryunderground.org

Many of the poems included in *This Is Poetry Volume III* are re-prints from the following publications and presses. The editor of this anthology wishes to recognize and thank them for their contribution to the small press.

Aterark, Bank-Heavy Press, The Beat Museum, *Bicycle Review*, *Bozalta*, *Chiron Review*, Citizens for Decent Literature Press, *Clutching at Straws*, *COG*, *Cultural Weekly*, *The Dead Mule School of Southern Literature*, *Dryland*, *Dufus*, *Durable Goods*, Epic Rites Press, *Freeze Ray Poetry*, *Full of Crow*, *Generations Literary Journal*, *Gutter Eloquence Magazine*, *H_NGM_N*, *The Journal of MALCS (Mujeres Activas en Letras y Cambio Social)*, *Luna Luna Magazine*, Manic D Press, *Nefarious Ballerina*, Nomadic Press, *poeticdiversity*, Punk Hostage Press, *Quill and Parchment*, *Rattle*, Rattlesnake Press, *Red Fez Publications*, Red Wind Books, *River Styx*, *Samizdat Literary Journal*, *San Gabriel Valley Poetry Quarterly*, *Spectrum*, *The Suisun Valley Review*, Turkey Buzzard Press, *Underground Voices*, *Word Riot*, *Zygote in my Coffee*.

Poems by Scott Wannberg have been included in this anthology with the permission of the Estate of Scott Wannberg.

C O N T E N T S

CONTENTS

C O N T E N T S

CONTENTS

A. Razor

Jason Hardung

Dustin Holland

Kevin Ridgeway

William Seward Bonnie

William Taylor Jr.

CONTENTS

C O N T E N T S

"I learned that just beneath the surface there's another world, and still different worlds as you dig deeper. I knew it as a kid, but I couldn't find the proof. It was just a kind of feeling. There is goodness in blue skies and flowers, but another force—a wild pain and decay—also accompanies everything."

— *David Lynch*

You In The Town
Cassandra Dallett

Where our burned brown grass blows with Swisher Sweets
and orange Cheeto bags the kids call Hot Chips
beg for them like crack heads searching for rocks.
The comforting rooster's crow
wakes us to helicopters and traffic jams
each murder more terrifying and awful
but the white folks keep coming
each week we spot a new one in our neighborhood
with their bicycles and smart cars.

The new colonizers
armed with flannel shirts, beards,
too many tattoos, and black framed glasses.
They farm corner lots and keep bees and for this, we are grateful
but the high rents they carry across the bridge with them,
the organic eateries, green bike lanes,
and café tables taking up parking spaces,
are bitter blessings.

Tenants find notice on their doors,
landlords praise this second coming in real estate-land,
farmers markets sprout up, and not so ironic art is everywhere.
But these idealist kids, they don't understand
the tribulations they peddle into.
The deep east outlands they don't venture in.
They can't grasp the reasons they are walking targets,
find themselves cold muzzle to temple
stripped of all their hip-hipster cash.

They think they're struggling, broke
but have never felt inherited desperation,
the day-in day-out eating of top ramen lucky to slice hot dogs
or dump Hot Chips into salty noodles.
Have never felt the whip of an extension cord on wet skin,
or lived in fear of enemies who only hate them
for looking just like them, fatherless and angry
strapped with frustration and bullets.

So many cold hard guns fill these streets
vegetables help to feed bellies and brains
but with no jobs and education the divide continues.

These cool kids landing here
thinking it's the new winterless Brooklyn
will cycle back to suburbia
when they find themselves staring down that barrel of hunger
flat black eyes, young, dreadlocked,
born of these streets, born in the struggle.

The Moon Lives In The Fat Of My Stomach
Cassandra Dallett

Inside me the eggs still come
sad fallopian hands wave no more
so many obstacles
fifteen years between us
would be nothing
if babies held easily to aging uteri
if we both hadn't suffered so much loss
baby the one pure thing I could give you
the one damned thing I cannot
I wonder if you truly understand
how I saved myself over and over again
filling my cells with blame
grabbed, spit on, rocks thrown at me on the street
by men
hands under my skirt,
fists to my teeth
just for saying
please don't touch me
I blamed only myself
my whorish leather boots, cat suits,
the types of men,
bad neighborhoods,
it was my fault when I hid fat lips
head down sunglasses disguising the purple of bruise
what I wanted was simple
I didn't know it existed
had never seen man as friend
never been treated as a friend

male friends I usually fucked first
to get it out of the way
there were a lot of casualties I swept up
and carried with me
a heart of scar tissue
like the surface of the Moon.

I wish I'd made lists of funny shit my son said in the car
Cassandra Dallett

how I wish I wrote then
all those profound questions he railed me with
when I begged for a moment of silence
to be alone with my own ragged brain in traffic
when he said Mom don't say fuck to the cars
when his nose was bloodied because he wouldn't stay in his car seat
and I buckled him beside me
where he climbed precocious on his knees
me screaming sit down
smashing the breaks and trying to explain the blood
to the day care lady he loved, Miss Khan.

I saw a call for submissions of poems about motherhood
wondered if I had any, was it really so long ago?
Do I remember nothing of his heaviness in my belly,
the knives in my nipples,
his hands that were tiny, then fat and square,
now long and lean.

We didn't have camcorders and cell phones to capture him small
I wonder if I documented enough
in nursing school they always said document, document, document
but that's just to cover your ass
I did scribble cursive entries of love through my pregnancy
in a flowery journal I listed baby names and intentions
names like Egyptia and Passion
and he said mom what am I going to do with that
I can't read that, we don't use cursive anymore

How he inherited the curse of my chicken scratch penmanship
but could use a keyboard almost since he learned to talk
how I showed him the ultrasound instead
his little fist raised in warning of the sweet hell he would give
the way he slept sideways beside me
falling asleep in his own bed and crawling into mine each night
to push me to the edge
velvet feet kicking my cheek.

Did I make him grow too fast with all my rushing
every countertop had to be crumbless and bodies washed
before I would rest
I did not know how soon he would walk out the door
head scraping the door jamb
How I would sit in his room fingers hovering letter keys
life of unwritten chapters stretching ahead
his childhood behind me and impossible to return.

Lust at the Cafe Formosa

Alexis Rhone Fancher

Once, at the Cafe Formosa in L.A.,
I saw the most beautiful girl. And
the best part was, you could see she didn't know it. Yet.
Didn't know how anxiously her nipples strained
against her shirt, or that her endless legs
and sloe-eyed gaze were worth a million
bucks... to someone.

She was a sway-in-the-wind willow, her skin
the pale of vanilla ice cream, her hair all shiny black
straight like an Asian girl's, thick as a mop.
She was maybe seventeen, on the brink, so ripe
sex exuded from her pores. She leaned against the juke box
fingering those quarters in her shorts' pocket
so they jingled like Christmas, the fabric
between her thighs stretched to bursting.

When her food arrived, the girl unwrapped
the chopsticks, lifted Kung Pow chicken to her mouth,
inhaled the spicy morsels. A long, sauce-slicked
noodle played with her lips and I longed to lick it off.
I'd been alone four years by then,
so used to it even the longing had long departed.

Then she showed up, all fresh-spangled, clueless.
If I didn't walk out then I never would. Elvis was crooning
Don't Be Cruel, but I knew she would be.
Girls like her can't help it.

White Flag
Alexis Rhone Fancher

On Edward Hopper's painting, "Morning Light."

No one paints loneliness like he does. Those half-clad women by the bed, on the floor, hunched over, staring out the window, in profile or from behind, always clean lines, such worshipful light. The gas station in the middle of nowhere, estranged couples on the bright-lit porch after dark. Even the boats sail alone. And the diners. The hatted strangers, coming on to a redhead, a moody blonde, all of them losers, all of them desperate for a second chance. This morning the sunlight pried open my eyes, flooded our bedroom walls. I sat alone, in profile on our bed in a pink chemise, knees drawn up, arms crossed over my calves, staring out the window. Desperate for you. No one paints loneliness like Edward Hopper paints me, missing you, apologies on my lips. Come back. Stand below my window. Watch me beg for a second chance. Downturned mouth, teary eyes, parted knees, open thighs, that famous shaft of Hopper light a white flag, if only you could see.

I Pledge Allegiance
Ellaraine Lockie

A hundred times to L. A.
over fifteen years
And always
the feeling of foreign
Like I've jet lagged
through a throng of latitudes
Into a land
of encyclopedic disparity
Located somewhere
between National Geographic exotic
and National Enquirer grotesque

Homegrown tossed
into the Hollywood Bowl
of big time travel
Spun beside silicone breasts
bleached blondes and BMWs
in other-worldly wealth on the West side
Garnished with conspicuous
consumption and grams
of high-grade cocaine
Ingested in houses
that host guided group tours
Where my bottled water won't blend
with movie industry's oiled opulence
Congealed in its counterfeit
attempts at real existence

Found authentic on the East end
Where I can't mix
with multi-lingual incoherence
of a melting pot stew
Fear steaming from the sight
of street hustlers serving dirty-
needled dope to teenagers
And semi-automatics to Hell's Angel types
Alongside houses the shape
of shopping carts with addresses in alleys

Adjacent to an occasional artist
co-existing behind caged windows
and 2:00 a. m. clubs
Feral in a savage jungle
Where I'm a safari spectator
Subject to jeopardy in traffic jams
freeway shootings
and Rodney King scenes
An alien in my own country
Unconnected to anything outside
resident daughters and Disneyland

Until an American flag peeks
its post September 11 tribute from under
an oak tree hovering over a crack house
Tiny stars and stripes on a six-inch

stem transplanted beside
empty beer cans and cigarette butts
Other flags flapping frequent freeway fraternity
between the BMWs and dent fendered heaps
Horns blaring at *Honk if you*
love America bumper stickers
Slogans similar on flagged T shirts
slipcasing the fake breasts
Compatriot cats and dogs
dressed in red white and blue collars
I buy a flag-contoured cookie
from a street peddler
without food poisoning worry
And I'm suddenly at home
Tierra natal, bayan ko, la patrie

Narrow Openings

Francesca Bell

A constant dripping on a day of steady rain
and a contentious woman are alike. —Proverbs 27:15

It's hot. The clouds' soft faces
are closed, a billowing refusal,
and I want to quarrel
with my lover, who just sits,
risen dull from a bed we left
damp as horses run hard.
Hair hangs, humid and tangled,
on my neck, but he won't unlatch
the window, doesn't like the noise.
I don't like him very much.
I want to argue until anger splits me
like God did. I choose lipstick
to startle him, Ultra Violent.
He just watches, his hair still holding
the shape of my hands.
Raising my legs,
I let the mirror catch me,
throw him bare skin glistening
sweat. *Going for a walk*, I say,
slipping into the narrow openings
of sandals, smiling as anger reddens
his dim face. Down each block,
I think of him pacing
the closed rooms, stupid and lovely.
Face glowing, I am an August peach,
and my feet slapping the sidewalk
a dance as good, as constant, as rain.

Severance

Francesca Bell

—*for John*

I'm one of those men,
he told me with a crooked
little smile, reaching gingerly
across the space between us.
Men you read about
in history books, he said,
as his right hand, the hand
with one finger gone AWOL,
vanished into the darkness
up my skirt and crept beyond
my underwear's flimsy barrier.
It was twenty years ago. I was nineteen,
like you are now. I nodded
and pressed firmly against his touch
trying to figure
which part of him I felt—
whether it was a finger he still had
or the one he'd lost
that slipped inside me.

When I got back,
I didn't tell anyone.
Just smoked opium in some hotel,
bought myself a fur coat.
I felt like goddamn Jim Morrison.
I felt like—he paused, shifting
to where he could reach me
better—*like what I was.*

A man who killed women and children,
fucking infants.
He halted there, to see that he had me
at attention—*I killed with pleasure*
whatever I could. I cried out
at that, but was by then
too far to pull back,
and shuddered helplessly
against his maimed hand,
sure then that what I felt
was the part of him
gone missing.

People
Ellyn Maybe

there are people
who hold an abridged tablet
of the ten commandments
in the space between their teeth and jaw.

there are people
who come into a room
with stardust on their breath
like a lullaby of backward halitosis.

there are people
who hold the planets together
by clicking their achilles heels three times.

there are people
who skywrite
without an airplane
without a net.

there are people
who twirl a room
like a rodeo for the sheepish.

there are people
who have bowling parties in their pajamas
while the rest of the world
seems like a pin
waiting for an angel to step out onto the dance floor.

there are people
who seem to have eyeball upon eyeball
like gumballs in an arcade of vision.

there are people
who walk into a room
a thermometer preceding them.

there are people
who wear their weather like perfume.

there are people
who know the cuckoo is the state bird
of most states of mind.

there are people
who went to the same high school
and spent each recess
in the lost and found room
uttering their phonetic name.

there are people
who will have conversations
deep as deathbed soliloquies
and never speak again.

there are people
who make whatever street they're on
Telegraph Avenue 1964.

there are people
who write a shopping list
in hieroglyphics.

there are people
who look up at the sun
8000 times a day
and lack an eclipse.

there are people
who drag questions
from the tongue
like photos one second
before the crisp of a fire.

there are people
who ask nothing
and your heart sits like a blank check
in a bookstore that sells only elegy.

there are people
with a little past
behind their ears.

there are people
with a newscast on their eyebrows.

there are people
no matter how many apples they held
teachers resented them.

there are people
who ring many doorbells
but won't let themselves in.

there are people
who light candles half the week
and swallow swords the rest.

there are people
who memorize the footprints
made by the snow.

there are people
who dine on shivers.

there are people
who chew on icicles
all year round.

there are people
who pray
with the nostalgia of baseball.

there are people
who laugh at life
openmouthed like a kiss.

Parallel Universe

Ellyn Maybe

Sometimes I wonder if there are one million people
listening at the same time
to the same Leonard Cohen song.
the one that keeps people from killing themselves
It's a long playing record
It's a long song

Where do people play each other the songs that will keep
them standing when one foot in front of the other is more
myth than practice?

I once tried to play Beware of Darkness by George Harrison
for a friend,
cause its beauty and pain were singular at that moment and
I wanted to share
I wanted us to hear as close as we could the same thing and
make of it what we would

He said he heard that song when it first came out and ran out
to smoke a cigarette
We lost something in that moment

I listen to music alone, but I imagine there are sharp notes
bending the backs of the universe into more flexibility,
more love,
more tenderness, more a capella chiropractors

Somebody is strumming 3 basic chords and
somebody will live through the night.

Cursive

Sharon Coleman

The V of my legs over the black seat of his Yamaha
doubles the V of his legs as tires grip asphalt, pull us

forward, leave behind an almost hundred-year-old
apartment house built for survivors of the quake

behind a used Cadillac dealership. We weave through
downtown, past droves of high school students,

an encampment of homeless, scattered office workers,
city traffic, and leave behind the grid of city flats

to snake up hills. He points to the corner where
he took a spill a week before in January rain, and

I feel asphalt—steamy in winter sun—close to bone-
breaking acceleration that leaves behind my signature

on withdrawal papers. He says this is more real
than the classes I just dropped—I no longer trusted

the words I couldn't even put onto paper. I don't
believe him. Yet I tighten my thighs around the cycle

as it grips the road and jets us forward, now past
Spanish-style homes behind wild landscapes,

dripping leaves. Past eucalyptus shedding swaths
of bark and scented oxygen, threatening to fall

from the rain-loosened soil beneath shallow roots.
The steep climb evens out at the road along the hills'

ridge, below squares of metal and glass, bay waters
beyond reflect strewn specks of afternoon sun.

Past us speed four Hell's Angels, their red-brown
hair streaming. We turn into the forest where

the road twists through evergreens, sometimes
a skeletal winter branch that drips darkness, cold

for lips underneath the helmet's mask. We then dip
toward the hills' eastern slope, a valley dotted by oaks.

Here we stop. Walk out to a stretch of low hills,
tall grass—mud firm under our steps. I look

further eastward, over round hills tinged pink
in diminishing light, to where my great grandfather

signed an X under his name for a farm in the shadows
of Mount Diablo. Look into dusk of gnarled branches—

brown against grey then black against dark blue—
oaken cursive arms to climb and lay my body in

until flesh and bone marry living wood, and exile
soaks into roots and soil below. We walk back.

Pull helmets tight over our heads. The cycle's light
beams paths between dark trees, small glimpses,

like a reversed writing over roads and leaves.
Alone at midnight and blanketed by darkness

I'll pour this writing into notebooks not to be
opened again for years—ink of heartless words,

half understood, soaks into pages are bathed
by slits of lights through the apartment blinds

from the dealership spotlights below while a man
who walks the streets screams curses into his night.

Castera Street

Lisa Douglass

On the floor of Nana's house
—I was sent there because my mother couldn't handle
my sister and I—
I played with dolls and gave them voices and names
Nana disappeared into back rooms
or outside to water succulents
the plastic pitcher with flowers on the side
I never followed her unless I needed something to eat
she sometimes made me those cookies
white powdered sugar over crescent moons
Later she forgot my name
called me, Janet, her dead alcoholic daughter
I thought that meant I was bad
but had no one to ask
Sometimes I sat in the avocado tree
watching her love her plants
bending down, dusting them in her sun-hat
I wondered why there were no other girls on that street
I asked Nana— she said it was time to water the garden.
When I slept there, I stared at the alarm clock with
glowing hands while
Nana drew letters on my back
and I would guess what they were
Sometimes I would confuse X with T
because of the angle.
Nana slept with toilet paper pinned to her hair
and I asked her once
"When you die can I have this?"
holding up a beautiful watch with diamonds for initials

I didn't know what I was saying
She walked out of the room
Her short heels clack clacking on the hard wood floor

Harry Dean Stanton

Lisa Douglass

It was hot outside
I was working at the Grill in Beverly Hills
After work I slid up to the bar at Dan Tana's and ordered a beer
Harry Dean Stanton was there drinking me one for one
He drank silent like me
I said, "you must hear this all the time
So I'm reluctant to tell you
But Paris, Texas is one hell of a film
And you're great"
"Yeah."
"Did you hear me?"
"Yeah, I hear you"
He said it like I had found out he fucked his sister
But then
I ordered us both a round
And he looked into my eyes
Grateful
That someone had bought him a drink
"What was your name, dear?"
I told him
"Thank you for what you said before, sorry I'm such a prick."
"No problem, I'm a prick too"
That made Harry Dean laugh like he'd found his hero
Me, Harry Dean's hero
I told him some mean stories about how I was torturing my boyfriend
But this one deserved it
I told him about getting run off the 101 freeway
And then he knew I was telling the truth
When I showed him the papers from jail

And he asked me if he could help by calling the house
I said yes, it might just do him in
He keeps threatening suicide after the meth wears off
He agreed to take my number and call a bunch
And we laughed some more
Some other guy
A guy I didn't even know, but wanted to
Walked by and handed me a bindle of coke
"Help yourself. Just don't be a pig," he said
The bartender thought I was a good girl
And gave me hatred eyes, like don't do coke
You're mine
But I gave a look back
One that said, who are you?
We're friends like this
I pay you for drinks, but mostly they are free
Because you think we might fuck
But it doesn't mean shit
So I slid off the stool and went to the can to
"not be a pig about the coke"
Then, I came back and Harry was crying
Telling me he loved me
"You don't love me, you're drunk."
Okay, I remember, he said
Looking for love in my eyes but only finding weakness
I put my arm around him and said
It happened to me too last night, I forgot who I loved
And then I ordered two more drinks
To help us remember
Who we really were

The Art of Not Touching

Lisa Douglass

Behind my couch is a table, metal and polished
blonde eames era wood
shoved there for lack of room
when it got here–I used to put our meals on it
on black and white Chinese plates
I cooked tacos
I made lemonade
I had to find the color of your eyes from a photograph
we sat on silk pillows and forgot to hold hands

You told me you didn't like sex as much as making art
and since you don't make art, where did that leave us?
You wanted me to know
that you loved me though you never touched me
I've never known a man to make excuses for not fucking
A man who makes you kiss without tilting your head
I put the table behind the couch
so I don't have a reminder of what it looked like
sitting together, not touching
Later I learned you used to live on Pearl Harbor
swam in and out of sunken battleships
dressed like Ace Frehley in Ramona California
I also learned you play chess —drink tea
read science fiction and Creepy and Eerie Magazines
I didn't know that then
just that we stopped kissing
and that's all I do with your replacement
His eyes are blue.

The Burning
Lisa Douglass

And there are other reasons I burned the mattress.
I learned to sleep standing up against the wall
The moon cast a shadow on the mattress
of the both of us when we were children.
You were in your bug phase
The one where we researched the bugs that could exist
in a house with no couches, no tables.
You told me, "They smell like cumin."
But I couldn't smell it
We checked our bodies
Cleaned our couches
I still have the vacuum cleaner
It was 400 dollars.
You were married, that's the one thing I never say
It was a girl who worshipped me
Her name was like mine, Elise.

love song # 6 ["Soma"]
Alexandra Naughton

I want to smother each other in everything we see so much that it feels like nothing. I want to build walls around us together so that it's just us in this small sheetrock space sheltering each other, and we're intertwined, and we can feel every breath, and every whisper, so every movement makes me shake, and we can just look at each other and the drywall. I want to wrap ourselves in one another like we're one person and not even dusty daylight will come between us so we're sticking and stinking and we're parading around so people will be like "what the fuck was that?"

I want to envelop each other, like 47 guitar tracks layered one on top of one so we are just crumbled paper bags and comic books stacked on the floor.

Anxiety

s. Nicholas

I have to pee
and I'm dreaming
and in my dream
I'm in L.A.
I run from my date,
frantic to find release.
A sweet elderly couple
ushers me to the rear
of their shop where
the old man
sprinkles pine-y cat sand
on an ancient mattress
just for me.
I squat
and try my best
even though the six
naked bodies
wriggling together on the bed
are quite distracting
and my date has shown up
with a group of friends
to cheer me on.

Under *Douche Bag*

s. Nicholas

List the guy who tosses his soda can out of the car on the freeway.
List the guy who tosses his beer can out of the car on the freeway.
List artists who randomly slap paint globs on canvas and then charge $300 for it.
List Andy Warhol.
List the guy who wears a zip up sweater.
List the guy who doesn't wear an undershirt under his zip up sweater.
List some of your mom's ex-boyfriends.
List the chick who asks the prof an irrelevant question three minutes before class ends.
List the prof who gives her a ten minute irrelevant answer.
List people who replace their spouses with their kids.
List people who replace their kids with a heroin habit.
List estranged couples who replace their weapons with their children.
List revisionists.
List the bank that took your house.
List the politicians who gave the banks a hand up after they took your house.
List the chick who reads the book after watching the movie.
List the chick who watches the movie instead of reading the book.
List anyone who claims to have, or actually has, read Ulysses.
List anyone who saw Titanic in the theatre.
List anyone who saw Titanic in the theater for a second time.
List pushers who sell weed to sixth graders.
List McDonald's.
List old ladies who stroll on the treadmill while watching soap operas.
List old ladies who run you over in the Stater Bros. Parking lot.
List the entire dada movement.
List poets who write list poems.

List parents who change the baby's diaper at the beach and then leave it.

List BP.

List all Dodger fans.

List Chik-Fil-A customers.

List David Duke.

List the co-worker who said she was frightened when she saw a black man walking across the parking lot toward her.

Mission Street Love Story

MK Chavez

On 16th and Valencia *Esta Noche's*
Christmas lights blink all through the year.

Sergio, the outreach worker calls it
"Esta Nightmare"
& hands out condoms to women
who use to be men, who he'll fuck
after the lights have stopped their show.

There is cilantro in the air
& the sweet smell of muscled men
holding hands. I get hungry
watching the brown skinned butches
with their femmes.

In the gutter on the corner of 17th
& Mission, if you look closely enough
you might see a twenty dollar bill,
a collection of rotting teeth,
a small baggie of sticky yellow cocaine
to shoot along with your black tar.
Shards of green-night train-glass,
above it on the curb is a hooker's pride.
She negotiates a ten dollar trick
& if you look at her too long
she'll kick your ass.

And two school girls on 24th & Guerrero
roll up their skirts before stepping through the arches
of the Church of the Immaculate Conception.

One of them is pregnant for sure & the other one
might be & neither of them knows what hell
really means, at least not yet.

There's a new 99 cent store next to the place
where you can buy rosaries & first communion
dresses & the taqueria that's been there
for 25 years now offers vegan alternatives.
You can still buy crack
on the corner, in front of McDonalds.

Things haven't changed all that much,
you can still get all you need in the Mission,
but now if you want you can have a cute white guy
pierce you and slide a ring through your nipple
while he tells you all about his Prince Albert.

And if you find yourself alone at night. You can get drunk
with Lesbians at the Lexington,
have your nails done at the Beauty Bar,
eat overpriced tapas at Cha Cha Cha,
pick up a good book or a drunk poet at a used bookstore,
shoot dope in the bathroom at the Uptown,
get harassed by drunk frat boys, gang bangers
and hipsters all within a one block radius,
and when the pain & the suffering hits
you can bury your dead at Driscolls,
and mourn on the streets,
no one will stop you.

You can go away,
the Mission will always be waiting.

Convocation

MK Chavez

I always knew that I would burn. I knew it even at seven, standing in the Jehovah Hall wearing a Pepto-Bismol pink crinoline dress, my fat-knobby knees rubbing that rough fabric, the itch of that crinoline dress and a forced smile. The force upon me like damp fur. I could smell it, the danger of it, God, and the stink of anti-sinner. I was wearing a mask, a forced-slash of a smile carved onto my face, a thick sash wrapped around the waist, and the silk sash was falling, and unfurling. The banner of Jehovah hanging above everyone's head and a boy stood next to me, shiny, his hair greased slick, black as a seal, his eyes black diamonds, and his mouth red as fire. The banner expanded towards the crowd, pregnant with air, announcing "Doers of God's Word," and then deflated as if meeting the crowd was a disappointment, the letters pulled into themselves, skinny and severe. Around us a congregation of black flies buzzed in the heat, the infernal pitch, the repetitive dull pulse that set off the cochlear nerve, pushing against the tympanic membrane, a constant drone, "Run," and "Tear off that dress," it hummed, and that growing itch grew, as did the urge to scratch. The boy leaned into my ear. The heat, the buzz swirling around me, and the heat emanating from his breath, volcanic, erupting into sound, "Let's go to the pool. Do you have a swimsuit?" And before I could answer he had fished the answer out of my eyes. "It's ok, we can swim naked," he said. He swallowed my hand in his, sweaty and sticky, like how I imagined a fly's legs might feel, when they rubbed them together, recalling their last meal, considering the future of the eggs they've laid.

You're Like A Burning Building

Iris Berry

And It doesn't matter that you made me so crazy
It doesn't matter that you are certifiably crazy
I think about your arms
and how the life force just pulses through your veins
I could build a whole life around your forearms
and the lines in your face,
how beautiful you are
even as you are aging
you can tell
that you were drop dead gorgeous
at one time
and that women threw themselves at you
even if you were an asshole
which I know you were
because you had the whole world
eating out of the palms of your hands
as you stepped on their feet
and how you could always make me laugh
the kind of laugh
that just can't be stopped
and that comes back
hours and days later
when I think about it,
and how you always brought me flowers
and gifts
for no reason, just to make me happy
but you'd always say
now remember this for when you hate me
and how being with you

was one of the most exciting rides I'd ever been on
even on the scary parts
when I thought for sure you would
burn the house down
or when I had to visit you in jail
and how seeing you in prison blues
behind bulletproof glass
made it all make sense
It's a good look for you.
and how you could always bring it out of me
and get me or anyone
to do things we never dreamed of
we were all your puppets
weren't we?
and I still am
even when you call
at three and four and five
in the morning...
after being up for days on end
on yet another speed run
and every time you talk about
how you just want to stop
and this time you will
or what about the time
we sang Crosby, Stills, Nash and Young
in your air conditioned car
in stacked traffic
and purposely way off key,
"I am yours,
you are mine
you are what you are
and you make it hard,"

and you do..
make it so hard
yes, you're like a burning building
that I have to run from
but I want the burning building
to want me to stay
but you would never admit that
and what good would it do
If I did
in order to stay
I'd have to put the fire out
and we know that's not possible
yes, you make it hard...
you're like a burning building
but what a lovely way to burn....

Love Gets Buried

Iris Berry

Love gets buried
under bad days
in the trash
forgotten to be taken out.
And that one loose handle
on the kitchen cupboard door
that
no one
ever
fucking
fixes.
Love gets buried
under bills
and no jobs
crumbling buildings
and terrorism.
Love gets buried
screaming and muffled
under the sound
of alcoholic neighbors
who always win
because they're drunker and louder.
Love gets buried
and forgotten
under countless
unpaid parking tickets
lost souls for loved ones
and motel drug overdoses.

Love gets buried
under friends dying too soon
before they ever had the chance
of a fully realized life.
Love gets buried
under the heartless shuffle of HMOs
finding things that aren't there
and not treating things that are.
Love gets buried
under lost blood tests
and bad carpet.
Love gets buried
and sometimes love resurrects.
And sometimes
love just gets buried.

Road Trip
Ann Menebroker

(for T.C.)

Hell, go there, where there
is a long stretch of music and no
destination except to go there;
not even get there, but just
the going wherever going goes
when it needs no more sense
than a bat flying out of hell, its
blindness singed with the power
of speed, with the glory of not
knowing where the walls are
and flying through them.

A Literary Caution

Jessica Dawson

Do not attempt to
shave your legs while
reading William Carlos Williams
in the bath, under
the influence
of medicine stronger
than your sickness.

You will find that
poetry demands attention,
leaving legs bare,
bony knees and ankles white
and ripe for a lesson
in rank.

Your inner thighs'
softness is no match
for a well-worded metaphor,
which in itself is a metaphor
for something you are not
prepared to grasp.

Airplane
Jessica Dawson

I'm bent, knee to elbow,
folded into
an impossibly small space called "airplane."

The man in the seat beside me is obscenely obese,
his rolls spilling
over the armrest
into my non-existent personal space.
He's viewing my cleavage
from his height advantage,
pretending to read over my shoulder
(which would be infinitely more polite).

His eyes are like
molesters' fingers
and enough to make (even) me shudder.

But the promised deviance
at the end of this
sweat-addled misery trip
is well worth the temporary suffering.
Visions —
a near-stranger
finger-fucking me over pillows,
wet panties lost in the
devastated sheets of
the XYZ hotel...

I'm sure my neighbor can SMELL me,
like a needy dog.
He's breathless and stutters,
inconsequential small talk — the weather, the cabin service.

I'll climb out of my body, sure as shit,
and leave it for him to
rake across the coals of his
lechery.

Navajo Boy
Jane Blue

He lived with Mormons
in California, he had
never seen a bicycle, he
missed his pony, the
Mormons wanted to
give him an education
out of the goodness
of their hearts, but
he resisted schoolrooms
as after the desert
they were too small.
I can still see his
square solemn face
in my kitchen, black-
rimmed government
issue glasses protecting
him somewhat, thick
lashes sweeping
at the lenses. "I am
an artist," he said;
he was eight years old,
come to play with my son.
The Navajo boy learned
to ride a bicycle easily
but as he flew hunched
down the hill, dragging
his whole leg for a brake,
he tried to imagine
a pinto pony under him,

sagebrush on the wind,
and could not, he
returned to the reservation
for he had a choice: it was
what the Mormons
called poverty.

Takes to His Bed

Sheila E. Murphy

He remains a modest man with wit,
who window shops relationships.
Not one inch of glass appears
transparent. Only the darkened image

of a self, après
relentless twitching
away from bedtime, beds
in general. He drives a hearty

vehicle into alleys,
where signage enumerates
the ordinances broken
by way of sitting still.

He taps messages into
the cloud, retrieves
a tapping all his own,
redeems a noun, a verb.

Playpen
Sheila E. Murphy

Young father, tall and seated
on plush grass in the front yard
frames a child in yellow dress,
whose stance is new.

She steadies on his knees, his feet
as fences, and looks out
at green, street side.
It is impossible

not to notice them, devoted
man protecting a half year
of life, learning to plant
one foot amid growth.

All windows face the rainless
afternoon. Clean light,
a few cars, and boundaries
almost invisible, apart.

(sympathetic muse)
John Macker

chased my loco dog Ruby half way across the *llano* today
until her tongue hung all limp, orange and sloppy from her panting
skull and I heard from Guillermo and Mike in Denver while listening
to Howl by Black Rebel Motorcycle Club and outside, spring wrapped
the land in rusted barbed wire and red dust. There's a fire
in my soul where true religion used to live, (due to a sympathetic
muse) just as you can smell roses where the nooses used to be. At
my age I don't have to be consistent, just clear, and the
occasional sympathetic news from the gods claims I'm
getting older, but no wilder and that friends are secrets you tell yourself
when you're lonely. According to this next song, "Devil's Waitin'",
I believe them.

August in the Spanish Earth

John Macker

These are the dog days of summer,
the heat has formed unholy
allegiances,
Lorca the pacifist was shot
on an August day at the foot
of the Sierra Nevada,
he prayed sweat into his
own grave, his
murder unmarked and late for his
funeral that never
showed up. We
leave memory to the
indigenous ghostliness of
the bones,
to these last days of deliberate warmth,
the field overgrown,
the orchard harvested,
the fallen peaches rot and sweeten
the air
and the last of the deliberate
angels give each other the first
of Last Rites,
but the words have risen and
wandered
away forever in time
from the Spanish earth.

Midwinter's day

John Macker

—*after d.a. levy*

I.

We finish our chili verde,
frijoles, a twelve dollar bottle of
vino, you can hear the ping of our
glasses across the universe.
We've been here before,
just her & I, another night
on the discomfited planet,
leave the one or two things better
left unsaid,
unsaid,
the wine is summer warm,
we relish its sincerity, we
progress gingerly from emotion
to emotion & in the ambling
circuitous nature of things,
come back to each other
on a deep starry black
                    night, when the
fire in the old Scandia
sizzles & pops,
              the sage
cross on it smokes so
slightly, its aroma tenders reflection,
an antidote to even the
subtlest of estrangements.

II.

Before the wine's gone
the underground horses & old
warriors shaking death rattles
will rise
          & take a wild last breath
ride with the devil across the
terrain of
absolute solstice darkness
called the poem,

the
humpbacked
universe will return to earth the
children taken too soon by guns,
Mexican wolves will laugh
at the moon,
no Mayan apocalypse now,
this certain slant of light
reveals mystery over form,
reveals poet
d.a. levy lived to be an old man,
his longest night collaged with peace
moonlight & words,
                    his
hometown
Cleveland cancelled its NRA
membership & invited all of its
Indians
home for Christmas.

Crisp
Michael N. Thompson

There's mold on the radiator
And oxygen seeped out
Of this wonderland
A long time ago

The night rapes
Those who wear halos
And a string
Of rag doll bodies
Who come searching
For salvation
Find out too late
There is no solace
In fame's bordello

Angels lie dying
Curled up on the pavement
Scarred from years
In a fierce dreamland
That drinks blood like wine

The revolution will be televised
And those surgically altered
Will melt from the sun's relentless glare

Swine by the bushel
Dine in an Elysium
Caked with more tanning beds
Than coffee shops

And the guard rails
Surrounding frail boulevards
Are chalk-marked
From those who've crashed
And burned to a crisp

While Writing Poems in Russian Hill
Michael N. Thompson

A blonde with legs
Up to her throat
And a mouth
Made to pleasure
Spends most of her time
Fending off men in suits
Trying to be
Her next sugar daddy

A couple of street dwellers
Check the trash can
Outside of the coffee shop
Every 10 or 15 minutes,
Hoping all the while
To find something
That will prove
To be valuable

There's a gym nearby
And the women
In tight spandex
Who swing their hips
While scurrying
To their workouts
Make me grateful
That I have
A window seat

A brown headboard
Takes up most of the space
In a homeless man's shopping cart

It must be a bitch
To haul that thing around

Soliloquy for the Vain

Michael N. Thompson

Virginia found solace
In other women
Despite a marriage
That she worked hard at

Once the medication failed,
She stood in the river with smooth stones
Bursting from overcoat pockets
Until ashes were scattered
Underneath the elms

Ernest's family tree
Bore branches of madness,
But this stubborn boozer
Was still a master storyteller

Depleted and delusional from shock therapy,
He discharged the chamber
And found himself between pine trees
In an Idaho cemetery

Sylvia's lust for death
Reared its ugly head
Once her father left
And getting drunk on Yeats
Only seconded the emotion

After putting the manuscript of Ariel on a table,
She sealed the room with tape

And laid her head down on a blanket
Until both the oven and her lungs
Filled with gas

Anne planned her demise
At three in the afternoon
When her purse got too heavy
With sleeping agents

When she was found,
Her lips were cherry red
While exhaust fumes and the radio
Echoed in her garage

(untitled)

Ryan Snellman

I spent a few minutes yesterday trolling the internet for you. Finding nothing I faded back into half remembered memories. I know you wanted to love me. Even after that night I beat up that abandoned car with a sledgehammer and you looked straight into the emptiness I could become you still cared. The way you would look at me with those eyes searching for something to hold onto; something to pull closer. That last day saying goodbye not wanting to let go is the only decent memory I will take to my grave.

One year I fell in love
Ryan Snellman

A desperate mad love
Each day was longing
To see her one more time
To feel her, to know her
To see the light burning in her eyes

One year I fell in with greed
A lust for money
If only to know power
A salacious hunger for control
If only for ones own destiny

One year I was mad for words
Mad to consume every idea, every thought
Mad to fill the empty page
With prophecy and poetry
Drunk on the idea I had
Something to say, something to add
To this human collective

Tonight, I fall for madness

In the low evening light

Ryan Snellman

I find myself whispering your name
A saxophone singing slow tender rhythms
Is that our song?
Or is every soft and subtle melody in you?
Drawing near
A faint implication of gin mixing with lavender perfume
Delicate caressing fingers
Moving in for a consuming embrace

Dancing with the ghost of your memory
I find myself humming the song
Of your beauty

Spring
Ryan Snellman

All these years later
I still dream of you
A day in the park
Late spring
Under that tree
Hiding from the sun
Half asleep
You
Tracing secrets
In the palm of my hand
Whispering a universe
Of desire
In my ear

The Serv-Well
Paul Corman-Roberts

It all starts with me coming home from the telemarketing gig, off the BART station at eleven every night per always, and then on up the Hyde Street wind tunnel for six blocks to the Serv-Well corner liquor pusher for an overpriced quart of milk and a can of raviolis at Ellis Street when a brother in front of me the size of a brick shithouse strolls five, maybe six paces out into Hyde, then whirls one hundred and eighty degrees on a dime at the sound of some shit talk and the bark of a forty-ouncer smacking off the sidewalk; another brother a quarter of the block down Ellis throwing down the corner liquor store gauntlet; two young men about to get it on in the heart of the one and only Tenderloin and adrenalin ripples out from the intersection, pushing uphill, rolling downhill and crawling toward the back of every alleyway evenly over a three block radius and it's all going down in front of the Serv-Well Market and I gotta go, yessiree I gotta get myself right the fuck across this here traffic, right across this here street and never in my life have I been so happy to see the gorgeous desolation of O'Farrell Street while pistol shots don't sound like they do in the movies (PA-CHEW! PA-CHEW!) but are a pop popping percussion that leaks around street corners and boxes in my ears while I hole in against a cleft in a brick wall only to find myself with an older, darker sister with canyon deep wisdom etched in her handsome jawbone croaks out "awshit, fools is gonna be dealin' out they dyin'" right before taking a gi-normous hit off of a tiny glass pipe, then gripping my shoulders while throwing her left leg around my waist and thrusting her tongue deep into my tonsils, allowing her coke washed, E & J flavored crack-hale roll into and overflow my sinuses leaving me heated, swollen and eager; leaving me wanting nothing more than to pull this smooth slab of loving neuro-electric carboplasm, deep inside of me until my wet has somehow consumed her wet but my ears pulse with the bastard cosmic hum of the ether and the distant pop-pop-pop, which caresses me warm, safe and sexy in the piss baked concrete smell of O'Farrell Street where I dream the creamy dreams of the possible for a period of time I cannot measure, but which only ever ends with me prone and alone in front of the stark, steely gray judgment that is the entrance gate to my apartment building...miraculously with keys, wallet and change somehow still in place...miraculously with my cock still dry and comfortably secured inside still zipped up Levis...miraculously with the sickly orange streetlight pall of O'Farrell Street completely abandoned, and every storefront bolted down and tucked snug against each other till the coming daylight, including, I am quite certain, my quart of milk and can of raviolis safely ensconced within the Serv-Well market.

A Murder In The Strip Mall

Paul Corman-Roberts

The king and queen
Of Best Western
Room 215
Everything strewn:

Surveying
The shopping center landscape
Psychic lust
acting out
at the family reunion

Varied shades of desperation,
Agendas ducking into
Back room charades
The hot new gossip
Counting out loud
Collateral emotional obligation

The consumers have abandoned
The parking lot in their wake

A scattered murder gorges
At the afterthought buffet
A Smorgasbord of discard
Framed by ramshackle dreams
The duct tape convoy of
Hollow drive-train eyes
& mobile methambition

The murder returns tomorrow
For their annual disillusionment with
An aborted consumer holocaust
A new feast of bitter sweet taunts &
Mockery, the kingdom of 1000 years
Once more denied the crows
999 years
11 months
And 30 days

Teeth In Fog
Paul Corman-Roberts

In the midst of a furious fog storm I left approximately one quarter of my facial wrap all over Hawk Hill Road, distributed generously between the handlebars of my one-speed roadster, & no one for miles. A quarter of my identity strewn about a lonely, lovely country road and you never realized how much teeth look just like little white rocks sitting on asphalt, mist particulates desperately trying to fill the space between them. It was a hint of course. One can never be stronger than the ground they stand on. This lesson is taught at every street corner.

The Liberal Who Lived In A Bubble

Paul Corman-Roberts

Flyover country is
closed for repairs
under reconstruction
this morning fading beneath
long cumulus scaffolding
haphazardly bolted
to the Sierra Nevada
ground Line
stapled by tornado
shaped reinforcements
over the continental crack

One can't help but wonder
if it exists at all
if it isn't just a vast hoax
perpetrated by CNN
to fill in the empty spaces
where advertising just doesn't matter
in this dreamy ludicrosity
until the long vacuum bubble
touches down in

Kcst-louisnash-vegasville-chicagorleans-atlantimore-brookyork

& the downtrodden
& the dreamers
& the hustlers
& cnn
are all still there

when flyover country isn't.

Bare Foot in River Mud

Bill Gainer

You never believed
in the magic,
did you?
You thought
plowing through time
would take you
places.
It won't,
hasn't –
never will.
It's the magic
only the magic
that gives the birds
flight
the stars their wink
and fills the heads
of dreamers
with dreams.
There's nothing else
to be said.
You should have
believed
you still can
there's time.
Maybe you can kiss
the tail of a lizard
find a worn rock
to set her on

tell her you love her
and good-bye
in the same breath.
I know
it sounds goofy
but it's a start ...

Women I've Loved
Bill Gainer

Sometimes
you have to wonder
if Marilyn
ever got to
just sit by the
pool
alone
swimsuit
loose, comfortable
straps undone
hanging
hair messed –
not caring
what she looked like
smoking a cigarette
sipping gin
no Kennedys
no Sinatra
no Rat Pack
just sweet dreams
of DiMaggio,
red roses
and some kid
from Santa Cruz
sending her
love letters ...

Another Time
Bill Gainer

When I used to drink,
which was considerable,
I'd tell stories.
I loved telling stories.
Like the one about the guy I knew
who knew a guy, who knew a guy
that could have been.
You know how that works
it just piles on to itself.
Then there was this woman I knew,
had three toes on her left foot
and no thumb on her right hand.
Something to do
with an horrific bowling accident
and a botched surgery ...
The whole thing
was settled out of court.
A nasty affair.
Emotionally –
she's never recovered.
They've removed that brand
of ball polishing machine
from across the country.
There's probably a few older models
still running up in Canada,
but when they wear out
they're gone too.
The company went belly up
a year or two later,

their new pin setting machine
kept dropping the nine
they couldn't get past it
sales never made expectations.
Rumor has it
that if there was a decent attorney
in the county at the time
she'd have three prosthetics,
all working
and minimally noticeable.
But you know how corrupt
it used to be
everybody on the take.
Hell, she was just a housewife –
her husband never took her dancing
that often anyway,
oh there was the Christmas parties
with the guys from the plant
and the occasional wedding reception
over at the VFW.
And her thumb,
hell she just pushed a few tissues
in her glove when she went to church
folks just thought she had a gentle grip.
It was a shame about her mind though,
slipping away like that
and all the dope they gave her.
Christ, no wonder the kids turned wild.
The oldest boy had that trouble.
The army was supposed
to straighten him out.
That was an ugly deal.

Feral, I think they call it feral
the kid was just too far gone feral.
But that's a whole-nother story,
another time maybe.
I gotta go by the post box.
See if my check's there.
All this talking
dries an old man out.

Process #1
A. Razor

let in the fullness of it all
fear may block the necessary
so let go completely with all
the dizzying effects that
come with that
layer overwhelming joy over fear
over hope over anger over love
over grief over heat over pain
over cold over sex over piss
over hurt over lust over think
over blood over hunger over lost
over wander over all over lovers
over war over birth over murder
over sick over spasm over tears
over semen over feast over shit
over hugs over moans over laughter
again & again & again & again
until until until until

work with the words in essence
work with the sound in assonance
work the tempo in time and edit
rewind edit rewind edit rewind
until the reels smoke from
spinning wildly in your mind

now focus hard on to it macro in thought
 now step back wide shot of the big picture

grab a hold of something that you hate
 to keep it close
let go of something you love & never get it back
push out demons & angels alike
invite whatever walks by in the darkness
to come into your light
let it examine you
as much as
you will
examine   it
 truncate & expand
with assured vision
that this is your truth in total
every word in line in break in pause
in running thought as it slows to dripping
into droplets of sounds of phonetics of language
acutely aware of itself as yours in truth & style as it
should be
pass it on like this if you can & be ready to take it
back at a moments notice
to run it through the raw breakdown of the mill in
your mind
once more
to work it into something more accurate
 for the next moment
to be more mathematically correct in its estimation
of your
unguarded soul as it sits in the center (of?) your body
somewhere between your mind & your heart

telling on your truth as if to snitch you
out to the last love you can find
along the terrible road to
creation

now get to work
make something else
before you get caught
waiting for praise that
never meant shit to
the source of your truth
in the first place

Desolation Angels Fall Too

A. Razor

do you lose your place
or your turn around here?

do you gain distance
or lose space over there?

between is where your thoughts
take you into a lush jungle of feelings
that come with their own sensations
coming to life in arcing sparks of
electrical charges across states and
boundaries and deep into walls of flesh
that quiver and part in aching acceptance
to the ghost of christmas future in a balled
up fist with only your natural juice flowing
over scarred knuckles for lubrication

a self oiled cylinder head on a hopped up
love machine with no handles and a fast ride
across the grassy plains and past the crack
of perky ass cheeks to hit home at the crux
of the matter where the spark burns into
the skin and leaves its mark on purpose
so that it never gets lost this way again

you stand for it
too long for pain
too long for pleasure
you stand for it

again and again
outside of a box
that was never
a set up or
even set up

you are only broken if you fall
you only fall if you love
you only quench if you
drink this overflowing manic
jism down your open throat
and let it soak your heart
with milky good warmth

you are only bent if you
lean into the wind as it
blows away thoughts
as it pushes passions
down sideways with the dirt
in a tango that tastes like rust
on a blood filled moon in
a december night's last
glimpse of steel inside
fragile wings of wax melting
away like a heart made of sand
as it pours out its
last hourglass
into the wind
that blows it
all alone

this angel may never come
but the destination your compass
has directed your soul to take
is going down like a falling
tree in a forgotten forest
that has grown so tired the
second it was born as a
lusty seed for pollen
looking for an up
escalator to the
gun store with
a trigger
that works
both ways

Parade (in 2 parts)

A. Razor

1.

it all runs by so fast in an anxious millisecond
as fingers on triggers wait so long
for the idea of peace to be dressed
into another military action
as the leaders read off of the
scripted notes that forget themselves
as the power brokers rejoice at another contract, fulfilled
while the people wait on a prophecy that fails to congeal
into a working wage or a fundamental human care
as people are being reduced into sad shadows
over many long years of service
watching children go off to
die young in an act of faith
against the backdrop of the ideal
that inspires memories of patriots
while a small percentile
holds onto the keys to riddles
that have turned into plagues
for inspiration when it is necessary
for decimation when it mandatory
from so many centuries ago
up until the moment of war
all the time, right now

2.

the banners were unfurled in a dead language
before god was made real in the battlefield
the marching never stops by proclamation
the smoke is the platform for the speeches
that sound like horns, that beat like drums
the world is hurtling down the route
here to sound the alarms
here to raise the troops
once again into the breech
o memorial!   o memorial!
even the peacemakers
dream of overrunning their masters
once in a great lonely while
to see if victory is really so sweet
as the propaganda might say
but, for now
we either march forward
or simply watch the parade go on by
cheering in a fearful exuberance
crying in a dreadful remembrance
the fields hold so many dead
never accounted for
we are lucky we can count the winners
of the world's most celebrated
losing proposition, ever

Humbled By The Way The Road Has Been

A. Razor
for Felix

the skies smile down in agreement with hearts
eyes tear up a little as the distances get eaten up
here you are when you arrive in the open arms
 of a happy child
the road is rolled up inside you with every mile
 you have ever traveled
you have traveled to get here never knowing
 this was your destination
all the thousands of apprehensive hours
 filled with desperation
time ticking away with movement
 slowed to standstills
uncertain paths you might take in whatever way
whichever way
 however way
way after way
until you seemed to have gone way out
 of the way of all ways
the world always spinning underneath you
sometimes in your favor, sometimes against you
the directions were garbled or forgotten
but, the journey had to be made
now you let it all hit you
as your eyes meet the child's
this is where you were headed all along
you are right where you always
 needed to be
 at last

Copper

Jason Hardung

The moon rises like a dead fish to the surface. My breath freezes and floats towards the moon. One time I was in love and finally able to get over myself. We kicked trash on the beach. Her face tasted of copper, everybody else had blank expressions—a bunch of flattened pennies. Blood collected in my cheeks due to the synchronicity of it. I had never felt more human. I felt as I was where I was supposed to be. What if we are moving as algorithms? And the sun and the sky are pixels? Some scientists believe that the universe is a computer program and if this happens to be true then whoever or whatever is behind the keyboard is our god. Our god is a mouth breather who lives in his mom's basement. Our god loves Mountain Dew. Our god has worn the same shirt for two centuries. Our god doesn't wash his hair. Our god loves watching violence but backs down during confrontation. Our god can't stick up for himself. Our god loves pitting people against each other, against nature, against themselves. Our god has never been laid. The moon is a glare on our god's corrective lenses and love is a hologram— you have to look at just right, to see what it really is.

Small Silver Cross

Jason Hardung

Walking through the window of night
I carry a small silver cross in my drug
pocket given to me by a homeless ex-boxer.

I was seventeen and impressionable
and he appeared from the box car shadows
of the Union Pacific train yards in Cheyenne
like the spirit of Tom Horn
but with a limp black eye and Mick accent

I carry this cross not because
I believe in Jesus but because
I believe in shiny things.

The human heart sets into motion
the plastic bag levitating in a corner,
the addiction, the paper planes, the nickel barrel
between rotting teeth

she was my heroin, I was her bitch
she the hot devil
coursing through my veins, the blood river
and the canoes of native American warriors,
rushing ashore, have become more,
than the white man's folklore

it's a movement in my gut,
a battle cry an inevitable genocide

It's been four months and you are still
eating my bones with your disease

I don't give a fuck about the sun anymore
Whether it's up or down
if it shines on my face in the morning
if the roses never grow again.

I blow smoke in winter's face
pick up a stick from the sidewalk
peel the skin back with my thumbnail
and keep walking until I'm somewhere else
drop the stick so when it comes to
it has to start over like the rest of
the broken and the damned.

The Early Years 1973-2005

Jason Hardung

Today is no different from any other day.
I was born in Wyoming
demons came through windows at night.
I wore a cowboy shirt
and shiny cap guns,
my bangs combed to the side.
I hid behind toilets.
I was scared of the bell at school so
a black kid named Wilbur walked me out.
His mom called me the white devil
and I probably was.
There was a tornado
and all I saved was my plastic horses.
My parents divorced
and I became a little girl.
holding my dad's leg
until he pushed me away.
I weighed 76 pounds in junior high
but still believed
I could be a basketball star.
I became angry
I cut a hole in a pillow and fucked it-
it felt like the right thing to do.
I never kissed a girl.
I was scared of vatos.
I picked up a skateboard
they accepted me.
A lot of them are gone now
the rest are married.

I fell in love with punk rock.
I learned to fight
I felt love
I wrote poetry in math class
I started drinking
then came the drugs.
I moved to Omaha in winter
and came back in winter.
Arrested for concealed weapon
and violent and tumultuous act.
I watched sunsets over the Tetons
Fell in love with a southern belle.
She left as the aspens burned.
The sky was bigger then.
Ended up in Tucson with a duffel bag
and a three day hallucinations.
Saw the Dead before they died.
Found painkillers and 40 oz.
Lived in a bus.
Stopped writing poetry.
Found more painkillers
and killer cocaine
found a woman
my dad found a needle in my arm.
Bought a house
Couldn't get in Canada
found heroin on the streets of Portland
bought needles where Drugstore Cowboy was filmed
I was cool I was gorgeous

dope sick initiation in the back of a Volkswagen
Fisherman's Wharf Donner Pass
Reno was a blur
Started a band
Scored on Larimer Street everyday
under the clock tower
Denver Colorado
worked in wood factory
shot up in bathroom
employee of the month
Steve died
Nathan died
Mark died
handcuffed
broke my leg
the lights went out
shit in a bucket
cooked dope by candle light
lost my house
brother went to rehab
lost my cat
lost my soul
robbed motorcycle gangs
one morning I prayed.

Poem for Jay and Jake
Dustin Holland

it was raining in
the cemetery for
ancient infants
and half realized
ambitions...about 20
feet from where they've
been pumping dinosaur
juice out of the ground

the gas mask only sort of fits over my eye-glasses
actually
the gas mask doesn't
fit over my eye-glasses at all

he watches the
water pour off
the brim of his hat

everything red
white and muddy
and a bathtub full of
broken glass and cardboard memory

eddie goode-shaman conquers his demons

Dustin Holland

i met eddie goode-shaman
in the parking lot of
one of norman rockwell's
all-american diners
the kind where everything
is red and white checkerboard
borders and pictures of
norma jean smiling like
little girls sometimes
smile at their fathers
and some pretty decent
apple pie all things considered

he said

'all poems are basically
lost causes'

i said something
inarticulate about
never wanting to grow
up and then we just
sort of looked at each
other and smiled politely

i spent the rest of
the night cutting up playboys
w/ a bottle of gin till
the floor fell thru

and left me suspended
above dancing lights
magic and unknowns
pouring abundant from
the front seat
like:
one soul along
the highway or a
big check from
ups?

flying down the road
in the back of a gyroscope
the kid crucifies
his heroes on the
windshield.

innumerable sacrifices
to the star god and
his illegitimate children

now i'm bill murray's
reckoning stowing away
on rimbaud's trip to
africa. doing push-ups
and eating rice w/ hot sauce
till it burns a hole in
my cheek and the neighbor
kids can try to flip

coins thru it for good luck

i keep an inventory
of dreams in my
backpack and go
crazy thinking of
all the folks i
never got to drink w/

he says
'all poems are basically
lost causes'
and sets his car
on fire

you can hear
the metal frame
singing itself thru
the ozone

just on the curb

Dustin Holland

outside the apartment
taking the dog to piss

an ice cream truck
rattles by

the sirens start
going off

karl says that this
is what happens
when angels come
to visit us

we're (all of us)
standing in
the semi-circle of
asphalt reserved
for parked cars,
recycling bins,
and cigarette butts.
watching pieces of our
futures in flashes of lightning

and which of these
clouds have the guts
to become tornados?

before long we're

in the car heading
to where the sky's
greenest
hunting for angels

not that we'd know
what to do if we caught one

but that i bet
they're pretty

and some days that's enough

My Neighbor's Back Yard
Kevin Ridgeway

he pulls a cart along the busy boulevard
full of bottles and cans collected
from dumpsters and private garbage
I hear the clash of broken glass and
dented aluminum in his backyard
next door; I peak over the fence
and a waft of methamphetamine
smoke hits me in the face while
he continues to puff on a glass
pipe. He offers me some and I
decline, watching the eyes in his
head swim his pupils trying to
break free and dry off on the
hairy beach of his salt-and-pepper
eyebrows. He offers me the
last dregs of a forty ounce
King Cobra, a cigarette butt
dancing at the bottom
I just stare at him for a moment,
standing beneath an unruly
tree of uneaten lemons
surrounded by rotting fruit
and flies. I thank my lucky
stars for my own filth, which
I move back to clean vigorously,
suds against the sins please
wash away.

17th Street
Kevin Ridgeway

she bakes the French bread
in the backroom
smoking half a cigarette
underneath the 3 am moonlight
the back door ajar
massaging her hair
underneath her employee cap
adjusting her upside down badge

8am rolls around in a stupor
and she announces this French bread
is on sale into a stale old PA microphone
with a genius for wordplay
and a savvy for sales

3PM rolls along like the
morning didn't exist
and she pulls onto 17th street
with a wedding cake in her trunk
up to the winding hills
of Anaheim,
searching for the stray balloons

6PM approaches, time to
start counting endless
receipts and quirky scribbling
on them to make the bank
for the dozens upon dozens
of goods sold that day

she comes home for me to
massage her neck, falling
asleep with a lit cigarette
in her mouth
I put it out.

Medication Time
Kevin Ridgeway

We stood in a crooked line
that extended from the nurse's
station to the activities room,
dressed in our pajamas at three
on a Tuesday afternoon. We
peeled and scratched the Elmer's
glue skins from our hands in the
wake of arts & crafts group, where
I declined to create a self portrait
out of macaroni, instead laboring
over an elaborate beaded bracelet
I was going to give to the pretty
Armenian girl who overdosed on
New Year's Eve, having failed to
die like the rest of us had all
wanted to.

Nerves tickled my pumped stomach
when she kissed me on the cheek,
her packed bags in hand after she
scrawled her cell phone number on
the front of my Xeroxed Relapse
Prevention handout. I never saw her
again, but I was on top of the imaginary
world at the front of that line with that
bracelet hidden in my sweaty palm and
my mouth opened wide so that the
Filipino nurse could be sure I swallowed
my lithium, daydreaming about that

crazy girl mixed up with crazy me, both
of us far away from that ward of catatonic
lunch room Pictionary teammates in a
place where we would have more than
just the will to live.

There's Powder all over everything
William Seward Bonnie

theres powder all over everything
the ground is levitating
ive sprouted horns
thorny rose bushs encase these palms as i stare down movie star
wet dreams
the moabe desert would castrate before we saw anything
strong words for a plot boss with no cause
just paid by the hour, ten pyramids to a dollar bill totem pole
scour the city for another powder puff muff diver
ill be sky high by 8am, wandering around flea markets in the upper
saint clair township of north pittsburgh, pennsylvania
smoking marlbo menthols while I scratch my nostrils because of
recent deposits
I think its the vhs tapes, or the n64 games, or the 3 foot bong rips
this lifestyles getting more outrages
Ive been living on tv dinners and skinned knee antics, and placebo
cream & artificial sugar cakes
black water southern rituals not for the weak stomachedindividuals
mixed media stencils that are so ritualistic its rude to compare
anything to them
for the simple fact that lightning strikes the temple of a hardworking
middleclass
man
ruptured spleen in a hospital bed, and Im doin this

I fell down some stairs

(clears throat)

falling asleep in a past life
I was as honest as a Denver man can be
with half a brain, a roomkey and a whole ki
a nation of pirates who we ride with who sleeps in your city streets
dirty, dusty and on small doses of what ever our heads need at the moment
no chromotosing...youll never wish to live so long
beards growin and your listening to the same dead song day after day
because its the only alone time you can ever get
blessed be the boy who comes in ragged clothes
scripture doesnt even do it for me any more
ive stared down the lord and the devil and ive breathed a thunderous roar
boats exploded down in the river quarry and the sun quickly was drowned by the storms
summers lonely blues
dark purple hearts of tours and acts of heroism and noses full of heroin
Im near and trimbleing...close to the moons radiant glow
ripe with anticipation and hope
the night wont be like most...
the next smile may come with tears
its hard not to be yourself out here
city streets...city lights

Blowing Up
William Taylor Jr.

He gave my poems back to me and said,
these are okay, man, but there's a bitterness in them.
Bitterness won't get you anywhere in life.

Okay, I said, thanks.

It's simple, he said, you get out of life what you put into it,
everybody gets exactly what they deserve, see?

I didn't find that notion particularly
plausible or comforting, but I let him go on.

Life's a game, he said, you either get rich
or you eat shit and die, it's as simple as that.

I'd never thought of it in exactly that way,
but I figured he must know something
because he was 29 years old,
edited a magazine
and had a pretty wife and a big house
in Mexico.

I came from nothing, he said,
I used to starve in little rooms for years,
living on tap water and stale bread.
But I worked, man, I worked 'round the clock
and look at me now, I'm gonna blow up real soon.

I wasn't quite sure if blowing up meant

becoming really famous or going on a killing spree
but I'm assuming he meant the former.

When I blow up, he continued,
I'm not gonna be greedy about it.
I just wanna inspire people
and piss off my haters,
use their energy to fuel my greatness.
I'll be free while they work their shitty
20 dollar an hour jobs for the rest of their lives.

I wanted to ask him about those 20 dollar an hour jobs
and how I might get one, but he went on:

Anyway, he said, poetry isn't the way to go.
It doesn't pay and the only way you'll get famous
is if you rap it, you know, hip hop style.

Well, I thought, shit.

Me, he said, I get paid 40 cents a word for writing bullshit.
Memoirs, restaurant reviews, anything but poetry, man.
You just need to learn how things work!

But don't worry, man, you can make it, too,
You just have to work hard, every day.
You gotta write at least 2000 words every day!

It was 4 o' clock on a Sunday afternoon

and all I'd accomplished thus far
was drink four cups of coffee,
fuck around on Facebook and take a bath.

Real writers, he said, they figure out
the way things work and write all day
and all night until they blow up!

I thought about the writers I knew
and I don't think many of them understood
much about the way things worked.

Most of them spent as much time
in bars and jails and nuthouses
as they did writing,

but I guess they weren't the real writers
he was talking about.
They didn't get paid 40 cents a word
and I guess most of them would eventually
just end up eating shit and dying.

But they were beautiful in their way.
They had strange light in their eyes
and sometimes said wise and funny things
that helped me through the lonely hours.

Anyway, he said, I've wasted enough time with you.
I'm gonna go get some real writing done
and if you're smart you'll do the same.

I've often had issues with smart,
and ended up having a beer and another bath
while pondering things a bit.

Thinking about how it all worked
just made me tired, so I took a nap
and when I got up I wrote another poem.

The Defeated Armies of Ruined Ages
William Taylor Jr.

The grand and pristine indifference of the universe
is the only lesson you really
need to learn
after that everything else
falls into place
and you'll come to realize
that your broken heart
is a one legged pigeon
or the story the junkie
tries to tell you
as she clings
to your arm
on any number of nights
you've long since
forgotten
you'll understand
the failure of your life
and all your wasted hours
are not unique
nor are they punishment
for sins in this
or any other world
think of the defeated armies
of ruined ages
think of dinosaurs
and dodos
your sisters' stillborn dreams
your parents' lonely graves

think of everything forgotten
and ashamed
throughout the centuries
the dog on the side of the road
the wheelchaired whore
on Larkin Street
imagine every ignoble
and embarrassing death
since the beginning of time
and you'll begin to understand
that her scorn
is just the grey dust drifting about the surface
of some planet that will never
be named
and the last look on her face
just the silence that comes
at 3 a.m. after the sounds
of trains far off
in the night
have gone quiet.

The Burning Moon and the Cries of Owls

William Taylor Jr.

(for John Swain)

Each day we wake into the terrible
fire of our lives,
and much of us aches
to dissolve into the great
and wondrous sorrow of it.
But at the core of our hearts
lies a wild joy at the burning;
it pulls us like puppets
to any number of silly dooms,
and though sometimes we find
a temporary peace,
some awkward haven in which
to rest awhile,
our shadow selves never let us
stay for long.
Soon enough something sings us
back into the night,
back beneath the burning moon
and the cries of owls
in search of some new trouble
to be equal to,
pausing now and then
beneath dead
and dying stars,
hunched with hands
of blood and parchment,
trying to translate fire
into words,

all the while understanding
our failure to be predestined,
utter
and glorious.

a little short

Dennis Cruz

she'd been snorting coke
all night long
licking the last bit
off the motel counter
at about five thirty
in the morning.
check out
was at eleven.
she spent twenty minutes
snorkeling up
the chunks
lodged in her throat.
it was disgusting.
he thought about
fucking her,
then spent thirty two
minutes
struggling through
the porn pay-per-view
prompts on the
telephone ordering
service.
finally he managed
to get people
fucking on the television.
the fucking people
were synthetic
and depraved.

he moved in
to kiss her.
she tried to ignore
the foul
of his breath,
as he flicked
his tongue
in and out
of her mouth.
she hoped the
chunks from
her throat
would dissolve
in her stomach
to distract
her away from the
coming sun.
she told herself
it was time
for a change
but wanted
to go out
with a bang
she told herself
she loved him still
she told herself
lots of things
she could never

remember
in the morning.
and finally
they did fuck
and it was
fast and unmemorable
and more than
a little short
of a bang.

where I find terror

Dennis Cruz

In the eyes of the corpses
bitten by crows.
In the smiles of generals
sending flowers
sending flowers...
on the butcher's apron,
where the blood makes patterns
like beautiful constellations.
on the beads of sweat,
dripping from
a prostitute's brow.
beneath the janitor's nails.
in the meat
stuck between
the cannibal's teeth.
in the heart of love.
in the hands of children.
in the suffocating
arms
of god.

i dream of tongues

Richard Vargas

i'm sitting in a bar in China
one of those drinking
establishments built
overnight to cater to
the Olympics crowd
featuring beers from all over
the globe and that damn
logo in my face wherever
i turn

i'm looking for a couple of poets
we wrote a book together and
we're meeting for the first time

i ask the bartender
if he knows them
he turns around and
grabs a manila envelope
from behind the register
drops it on the bar in
front of me

i reach inside and pull
out two copies of the book
each one has a human tongue
nailed to the cover
drained of blood
bleached and stiff

each tongue is tattooed
in black ink with the image
of a single feather
the quill is sharp and pointed
the barbs have all the minute
detail of a da Vinci sketch

whose barbaric vision is this?
to decorate the tongues of
poets with the ability
to soar above the clouds

why is it so beautiful?

my uncle calls
Richard Vargas

he's getting up there
in years and lately
he's been reaching out
letting me know he prays
for me and hopes i'll have
the same epiphany he had
years ago when he was
in the joint and God tapped
him on the shoulder
told him to get his shit
together or else

but i'm not there yet
maybe i never will be
but it's good to know
he thinks of me even
as i remember the time

i found my grandma's
measuring spoon tucked away
under the bathtub in her house
where my uncles hid their
stash of nudie magazines
the bottom was blackened like
it had been burned with a match
a dark cloud gathered overhead
when i showed her what i had found

later, i watched as five feet of fury
backed him up against the wall
when he walked through the door
my tio never knew what hit him
as grandma gave him a tongue lashing
in spanish so i couldn't know
what she was screaming about
her sharp words slapped his
face beet red while he tried to
hide the needle tracks on his arm

that was fifty years ago
now he prays for me
i guess that makes us even

Seal Beach Summer, 1972
Richard Vargas

that's me
lying on my favorite
Budweiser beach towel
spread out on the hot sand
where the noon day sun
turns me into a puddle
of 17 yr old sizzle
and sweat as i stare
up into what i will one day
realize is the bluest sky
i will ever see

that's her
a 16 yr old girl who has
stepped over the border
into that land of the dark
and the mysterious where
the scent of womanhood
clings to her like a pair
of skin-tight white shorts
and a pink tube top
on a steamy Saturday
night

she scoots over on
her stomach until
our arms touch and
lying side by side
she reaches across

cradles my head
against her breasts
makes me dizzy
with the sweet smell
of coppertone as she
lowers her face within
inches of my own
pries my lips apart
with a warm tongue
that is a fresh stick
of spearmint melting
in my mouth

the spray from a crashing wave
cools my skin and somewhere
i hear the hissing sound it makes
retreating back into the sea

a nipple rises out of nowhere
flashes me before falling back
under the blue and white gingham
fabric of her bikini

seagulls circle above
serenade the both of us
with their wicked
laugh

economic recovery
Richard Vargas

on the first day of training they
show us a video about the company's
global responsibility
how they go into third world countries
lock up their supply of the best coffee beans
show the locals better ways
to grow and harvest
increase output
decrease cost

they are green, too
convince governments that
their national parks can still
be cultivated without damaging
the pristine sheen of a fragile
and timeless subtropical forest

workers are provided with childcare
for the kids so papa and mama can
both work the beans
picking and processing
sun up to sun down

then we see a woman
in the back of her simple home
proudly standing in front of an outhouse
she opens the door and inside is
a commode, the kind that flushes
she is beaming and announces to

the camera in her native tongue
it makes her feel like she is one
of the rich people in her country
as a goat emits "baaaah-baaaaah"
in the background

a few weeks later
out of training and on the phone
i'm taking calls from my
fellow countrymen who complain
about how lousy their five dollar
cup-of-joe tasted that morning
because it was too hot
or did not have the extra
caramel crunchies and whipped cream
they specified during their order
and when are we going
to have organic soy milk
available because if
we're not they are taking
their business elsewhere
and that kid you call
a barista needs to be
taught some goddamn manners
because they had to wait 10 minutes
to get their coffee which
made them late for work
and by the way doesn't
all this inconvenience entitle

them to some coupons for
free drinks?

the day isn't half over
already i have a killer headache
getting paid one dollar more
than the local minimum wage
to stroke a population that can't figure
out the right thing to do when
their kids are shot up
and massacred in the classroom
by gun toting lunatics

but has no problem finding
the time to call and bitch
about the real important
things in their lives

while the grateful woman
somewhere in Central America
is taking a leisurely dump in her
fancy toilet reading the
Spanish edition of the
Wall Street Journal

Wholesome Television Memories

Rich Boucher

I always hated that one episode of Little House on the Prairie where, after rescuing a seriously ill, unconscious Reverend Johnny Johnson from his runaway wagon in a blizzard, an innocent, down-on-his luck high school bully I once had named Caleb puts on the clergyman's collar and devises a plan to fleece the charitable townsfolk of Walnut Grove; I always hated that one episode where Florence was hired as the church's maid against the wishes of Laverne DeFazio, that one episode where Dan Mateo, the Alphans' botanist, started turning into a murderous, disfigured ghost while the Riddler got taken over by an alien manifestation, that one episode where Helen Keller taught Nellie Oleson how to do sign language in the cornflower field and I discovered masturbation, that one episode where they found azure and cerulean bones in the bell tower and it caused my mother to want to be buried in Hazelnut Grove, that one episode where Melissa Sue Anderson had a flat tire in a bad neighborhood and got harassed by a committee of Amish youths until Jan became allergic to Tiger and I had to run for student body president against the both of them, that one episode where Mr. Hooper asked Big Bird to help Charles Ingalls open up the store for him, that one episode where celebrated shaman Namutebi Okoro moved from Uganda to Philbert Grove and was forced to marry Laura Ingalls while I watched, while they all tried to drown me and my dinosaur in Plum Creek, that one episode with the suicide of my friend from school, that one episode with my parents' funerals, that one episode where my marriage disappeared, that one episode where I started having a hard time believing in God.

Makeup Tips for the Eye of Horus
Rich Boucher

I thought they were actually demons
so I let the Neanderthal out of me and howled for blood;
I started hollering and yelling old man phrases after them
get the hell off my lawn and all that
even though I live with my girlfriend in her ex-husband's house,
and what little lawn we have is barely enough for anyone to get off of;
I didn't know if they were Jehovah's Witnesses
or Jehovah's Door-to-Door salesmen
but I stood my ground Florida-style with extra pulp and bellowed,
bellowed even though I hadn't shaved or Axed my body
and today's modern alchemists symbolize resistance to change
at an elemental level
with a line drawing, laid on its side, of Lady Gaga
hate-fucking Emily Post into oblivion;
like a man dispossessed I chased those three or four youths
away from my front door
and yes, I'll still use the term youths even though I'm almost forty-five
and the WWII vet at Wal-Mart would consider *me* a youth;
it turns out they were the new religious tract salesmen
but they were not selling seventh day advent anything at all;
they were selling that I should like what MTV has become now;
they were selling that I should be ready
for the Syrian slap-chop apocalypse;
they were selling that I should start not knowing
the meaning of gender anymore
and in modern alchemy the symbol for fear of being wrong
about a new person's gender
is a line drawing, laid on its side, of a stick figure man in a skirt in a
wheelchair digging a grave;

they were selling that I should learn to speak
like the modern young people
and begin to become ambiguous, that I should begin
to be afraid of being exact,
that I should start thinking of asking for a clear, concrete yes or no
as being rude;
it was the best three in the afternoon ever and I had the day off;
I was just eating my cereal just in a t-shirt and just my boxers
and it was a dark and stormy night even though it was three in the
afternoon;
I chased them out of my cul-de-sac on that overcast Thursday
like I was St. Anthony and they were a pack of demons
and I was running them away from here, forcing them off of Egypt's cliff;
I ran after them past the open living room windows of my neighborhood;
I heard the soap opera women crying in the daylight air,
wailing like the witches in the olden-time movies,
weeping with all due loudness and inconsolable
because it seemed like there was no one who could remember 1985;
I heard the octogenarian infomercials asking *who was that masked man*
as fiery spit flecks flew out of my muzzle as I chased them
chased them chased them
until they were at last and forever out of my empty
middle-of-the-workday driveway
and in today's secret, modern alchemy, *the symbol for ironic dissolution,*
the symbol for precipitative collapse into your own first, base element is
a drawing, laid on its side, of Lindsay Lohan wetting herself
while trying to light a joint in a world-famous elevator.

Nighthawk Blues

Rich Boucher

There's an all-night diner on the corner of Green and Washington forever, a few blocks down, always, from the Diamond Tavern and I'm almost there. I couldn't sleep; I still can't sleep; I might never sleep again. I walk, exhausted, from my apartment in the Lexington district all the way down here. I get a few blocks from the place and I stop at the park near Preston Gardens and I look up. The sky is still there, but it looks like it just got there a few minutes ago. Some of the stars in the sky are just waking up, and some of the stars in the sky are just getting ready to go to sleep. I know I'm not a star in the sky; I keep moving, and the closer I get to the diner the more the streetlights go out, the less light there is and then after a couple blocks' worth of total darkness I see the warm glow from the diner pouring out onto the corner; I look in the windows and see a redheaded woman in a red dress having a cup of coffee at the red counter. She's beautiful but she isn't alone; she's with a man and they're deep inside their own conversation. I get it: this part of town is composed of my insomnia and wanderlust and I push myself through the door. It's ninety-nine cents for a Coke or a coffee here; it's ninety-nine cents for a dream on rye; it's ninety-nine cents to go back in time. I make the redhead's gentleman companion disappear with a wish and take a seat beside her. There's no sound coming from the empty benches on the midnight street outside the windows and I fall, holding on to every year I've ever lived, into the gleaming crimson of her lips; I might never sleep again.

Meeting Halfway
John Bennett

I changed my skin color for you. I polished my shoes and painted my fingernails. I drank warm blood and sliced a hole in my groin. I've done a lot of subtracting to compensate for the impediment that you see in my eye.

Isn't it time you do a thing or two in return, open a soft spot in your armor, something I can stick my tongue thru and melt your cold heart? Modulate your voice perhaps, take off that cheap lipstick? Don't you remember our first kiss?

Please don't go. Please don't dissolve into that wasteland where the desert sand stings your face and wild birds circle high in the sky.

Secret Rhythm
John Bennett

He felt
he had
more limbs
than he
knew what
to do
with &
thought
maybe he
was a
Krishna or
a Vishnu
perhaps a
centipede or
an octopus,
something well
endowed with
appendages.

"Bobby hon
are you
alright
in there?"
his mother
called.
"Please baby,
come down
to dinner."

"I'm not
hungry mother,
please
leave me
alone,"
he said
thru the
closed
bedroom door,
& she
went back
down the
stairs.

He sat
on his
unmade
bed in
the dark
with his
many arms
wrapped
around him,
rocking to
his own
secret rhythm.

Union Station
Laurel Ann Bogen

I needed a timetable
for my heart
it always arrived
too early
departed too late
wandered lost on platforms

I needed you
to steamroller the creases
I folded too many times
I was hurry and drag
beat slow
sync steps

I came in pieces
like cartons tied
with baling wire
you held tight
against the spillage
and random punches

Oh I loved you like speed
like fast exits
and jackrabbit starts

you held all the tickets
you opened the gates

it was 2 minutes to boarding
and we pulled out all the stops

Nothing Breaks but the Resilient Heart

Laurel Ann Bogen

—Poem On A Line By Anne Pitkin

Save this beatbeating
for you oh lost boy
oh youth when you called
me goddess and now
the yellowed pages of days
rip and tear like cobwebs
pulled through fingers
and I cannot face
my sluggard
thick thighed passions
that sway and creep
almost dormant as if
to feel were too much
and I want to say
No Nothing breaks
but the resilient heart
the corsage ungiven
its scent gardenia
and this woman
trapped in flowers
who dances below
your window is the same
girl who pumped through shattered
memory to that place the heart knows
and knows everything

A Little Death

Laurel Ann Bogen

each evening
before twilight
before starlight
before the yellow houses
pull their shutters
into themselves

I remember my own
small death
in green and orange
and ash white pills
each beautiful
each perfect
each swaddling my senses
in cotton batting
and antiseptic truth
junkie truth

I have died
these many familiar times
this comfort
pulls my life about me
with sleepy fingers
like a warm blanket
and rocks me
with soft lullabies

no mother could
ever be so diligent

so real
so mine

one
two
buckle my shoe

twenty years
of little deaths
have left me
silent and barren
as Mother Sleep
no longer waits for me
drawing a tepid bath
but instead
opens her starched white uniform
and smothers me in her ample arms.

Narrow Beds

Laurel Ann Bogen

The spare honest lines
of my girlhood intersect
with wood and linen
Corners neatly tucked
I dreamt alone
with a radio
under my pillow
to ease the nightly terrors
Vampires sucked the dark
Death coaxed slyly
like Southern Comfort

I dreamt alone
long legs became longer
sinew and joint extended
Terror shifted from vertebrae to groin
The womb drummed insistently
Rapists scuttled from street lamps

I hunted boundaries
chanted pregnant lists
of lovers and college lecturers
clocked the seconds
from impulse to scream
slept in sheets of wild control

The demarcation of form –
bed, body, dream –

the weight of cloth
bore me down

There was a limit
a finite space
my body could not slip away.

The Lovelorn Astronomer
Luivette Resto

After every heartbreak
grandfather would recite
the tale of the lovelorn astronomer.

According to grandpa,
the man fell in love
with the moon
one November evening,
hypnotized by her glow
reflected on the concentric ripples
of the Hudson River.

He loved the moon
even when she hid
behind onyx clouds,
her beauty only a sliver
of light in the nautical fantasies of men.

He slept in the daytime
so he could be with her at night
to read her verses
written in a new language
created from haste, lust, agony,
promise and compromise.
Whispered secret memories
never revealed not even to he,

sang ballads to the constellations
he renamed for her,

constructed syzygies
to keep her company.

I want to feel like
the lovelorn astronomer
one day, Grandpa.

No, Mi'ja,
you want to be
the moon.

Painted Walls
Luivette Resto

Possessed by the spirits of renaissance artists
I paint over walls

    beach sand hues over red delicious
    memories embedded
    in the irregular shaped corners
    of my bedroom   sanctuary   office
    mommy's special timeout place

and years of masonry experience
continues as I build new facades
hallmarked with est.-in-1983 bricks
based in shame carried daily
like my unborn child.

Shame wrapped around me like a *sabana,*
worn like my mother's favorite perfume
its scent enmeshed with mine
as I inhale and exhale
the toxicity of childhood silence

eat, drink, sit and talk with shame
like the siblings I never had,
fuck it until I get love out of it

forget it ever existed
in the palms of an alcoholic mother
and bruises on four-year-old skin

forgive the wife for not calling the police,
believing she was the dirty bitch
he claimed with each slap to the face
and bruises on thirty-four-year-old skin

stare at it in the mirror
figuring out how to let it go
like an offering
left on the doorstep
of the ocean.

Botswana, Beats & Bushmen
Luivette Resto

At the art exhibition
she overhears a conversation
between the curator and an ardent art buyer,
a clinical psychologist

who has returned from
her annual trip to Botswana
where the Bushmen extract trauma
from the body and spirit
with dance around a fire
warmer than blood.

The eavesdropper closes her eyes
and her feet move up and down
to an imaginary drumbeat

     ball to heel
     heel to ball
     ball to heel

memories of a father
typically forgetting to pick up his daughter
on a humid Sunday afternoon,
the itchy blue taffeta dress
incubating the seeds of rage and resentment
     what man will love her
     if the first one doesn't

memories of mom's car keys taken away
when she forgot she was the parent
after three rounds of Long Island Teas.

Memories needed the beats of Botswana
created from the hands of healers
trapping them in a circle of fire and music
where case studies don't exist.

Lesson Plans

Luivette Resto

"Mockingbirds don't do one thing but make music for us to enjoy.
They don't eat up people's gardens, don't nest in corncribs,
they don't do one thing but sing their hearts out for us.
That's why it's a sin to kill a mockingbird." Miss Maudie

Seventh grade fingers
discover the word nigger
as they dog-ear their favorite moments.

Refusing to say the word aloud
in classroom discussions
or write it on reading quizzes,
they rather say "that bad word."

For them Atticus became the hero
as we all wished he was
our father, neighbor, legal counsel, friend.
They rooted for a not guilty verdict but said
Tom's storyline was foreshadowed
the day he was born.
I don't know, but they did it.
They've done it before and they did it tonight
and they'll do it again and when they do
it seems that only children weep.

They shed a tear when Tom was shot 17 times
calling it brutal, excessive, and unnecessary
as my news feed becomes the embodiment of Sophoclean irony
reporting the 6 shots in Michael Brown's body
reminding me of Amadou Diallo's 41.

Our courts have their faults,
as does any human institution,
but in this country our courts are the great levelers,

and in our courts all men are created equal.

How do I teach
grace instead of fear
when a uniform approaches
or explain the paradox
of an all-white male jury of one's peers
deciding men's fates.

How do I explain rape and domestic violence
to fifteen adolescent girls
when Mayella points her shaky finger at Tom
as her father clenches his fist.
How do I teach that lives matter
when classmates in other schools
make the headlines as victims or instigators.

How do I create a lesson plan for empathy
when Boo Radley is isolated and taunted by his neighbors
like they are in chat rooms or school yards.

Most people are nice when you finally see them.

Sandra Bland was a mockingbird
Trayvon Martin was a mockingbird
Freddy Gray was a mockingbird
Tamir Rice was a mockingbird
Eric Garner was a mockingbird
My sons and daughter are mockingbirds
and thirty mockingbirds sing from these desks
when they highlight the lines:

You never really know a man
until you stand in his shoes
and walk around in them.

some days the shrapnel feels like cotton candy
Scott Wannberg

the best laid plans of mice and men and all in between
just arrived for a three day weekend show at
the community theater
the actors sometimes cut like shrapnel
but when you eat them they taste like cotton candy
be careful
eating too much of a good thing can lead to revolution and
pestilence
or so they told me when i got up this morning
i just sort of opened my right eye
and Armageddon claimed it was my friend
i just sort of opened my left eye
and the wounded deer all came running to my side
the best laid plans of would be presidents and their assassins
and all in between
just folded up their tent at the
community sing along
the notes sometimes slice one's ear
but when you go to claim you are the reincarnation of Van Gogh
they demand that you walk a straight line
straight lines are okay in their own time
but they can be deceptive
i walked a straight line for days
but my heart was crooked when i put my feet down
i sing this one for all our crooked hearts
learning to bend in whatever weather shows up
those wounded deer have all left now
they are making the scene
you've heard about the scene

it supposedly is everywhere we ain't
okay by me
no one will tell me when to fold my tent
no one will tell me when to turn my music off
we are our own scene
i walk a somewhat straight line here and there
not really waiting on anything
but if anything shows
i will be more than ready
to share myself with it

state of the world amnesia rag
Scott Wannberg

understudy unsteady, done busted his/her right leg
someone left the newly born language in a paper sack on
the porch
when we get there
if we get there
do they got a swimming pool there
we can wash off all the
would be blood
i never even lifted a finger
i saw you try to raise a thumb
but the weight was too confusing
and the maitre d' claimed the food would be late
when we get there
had to turn in the leaf
for pretending it had turned over a new
sure
they got good action scenes coming up
listen to the special features comment
nobody is immune
the sirens audition for late night anything
soiree then
bagpipe me effortless
chipped a tooth on the one and only
called out for clearance sales of clarity
they take the good people away and put them in tubes
can't believe it no sir
hold on my feet are beginning to ask for a raise
when my world gets there
when my driver's license gets up, steals a world, and

flys away
well, the arguments they are tired now and have
gone to bed
let's not roust them any time soon
we can go amiable maybe
when we get there
the lights will still work
all the video tapes of murdered folk
will burn up without a fire marshal needing to be around
and the busses
they will pick us all up on time.

The Good Germans

S.A. Griffin

The TV laughs at us.
We are fat, stupid and to the
left.

The believers are right.
Incapable of apology because
there is no apologizing for them.

The believers are my siblings,
my in-laws, a few close friends.

The gay neighbors.

My stepmother, ex wife's brother
and most all his born again family.

They have unshakable faith in the sainted democracy of guns
and sing the trickle down honey of money.

The believers believe that global warming is a conspiracy
cooked up by the Chinese on capitalist crack, President Obama
from Kenya on a hip hop prayer rug, Hillary Clinton from Benghazi
wearing a slinky red email sex scandal sifted from the medicated
tea of yesterday's news, a reality show for Christ starring Kellyanne
Conway as Miss Informed, along with a half dozen jittery sled dogs in
Birkenstocks that can see Russia invading the White House from their
disappearing backyard.

Early on in this dark movie about WWII I saw late one night,
a well-dressed, educated, middle class family
is sitting down to dinner.

Just outside, tanks are coming down their street.

As the father, nervously trying to comfort his anxious family says,
"No need to worry, the soliders won't be coming for us,
we're the good Germans."

There are no good Germans.

There are only Germans
in this movie.

And we are all
Germans here,
tonight.

What Comes Between

S.A. Griffin

The fingerprint ridges have crimson ink. They press hard
into the undulating landscape of wet dreams may come,
grazing the surface of a shaggy hope while catching the
curious fire of an animated skyline leaping inside the
kaleidoscope's oscillating iris, the images raging twice the
acceptable speed necessary to map that further hill.

My heart never was my own; I won it guessing the atomic weight of music
while singing happy birthday into the wind at a vagrant carnival for the
hard of laughing run by fairytale giants barking somewhere out there
where the numbers had me at hello.

I never stop yearning for the cold burn that comes with the breathless
altitude achieved when all the cylinders click in spontaneous glee
and the words come pouring out with the untouchable muscle of a cubist
pen bleeding expressionist kisses.

> I drew carbon-dated pictures of Mohammed with
> disbelieving ink on the inside of my cartoon eyes
> and then blinded myself with the news.

> I took pictures of lonely Jesus at the prizefight
> and called God a liar for fixing the game.

> I woke Buddha and killed him in my dream of flight
> along the road less traveled at the foot of a
> very large family tree where he called me cousin
> and thanked me for my kindness.

It is impossible to be alone surfing the long-playing seconds
held together by boundless shivering moments
compulsively etching their groove into the
dark roast stardust of your every pregnant thought
sounding the strawberry alarm.

There are no savior walls to contain the naked fear
or drown the eyeless grief
as all our crippled histories come marching home
in a never-ending forgiveness parade
playing love is a gun on their
blind guitars made of
velvet hallelujah.

What It Is

S.A. Griffin

—*for Todd Moore*

said The Kid is 3 score
and 10 and the lingering musk of
pussy tingling on the tongue of time
the poem dancing in the raw
like an outlaw
under some eyeless sun
and the feeling that
there is still something left
and juice enough
to get it right
between the lines
between the sheets
between the devil and the
distractions

what it is said The Kid
is the machinery of Dillinger's
opus magic poking stars into
the epic story of this godless night
working the duende big dick fearless
my great act of faith
as the poem dangling from
death's tree bleeding into
the earth like so many
lost metaphors flickering
in the back seat of a Chevy
made for fucking and a quick
getaway

what it is said The Kid
is one more dream amigo
one well placed word like a
shot in the dark
and the truth somewhere in the
winking eye of a great whale
on some lonesome highway
south of any moral
north you could conjure
while rimming the gold
off Billie's sweating peach

your hot hard
Thompson spilling
like a prayer

Variation On Poem 9 by Ono No Komachi

S.A. Griffin

while counting days
    the blush of roses faded
and their petals fell
    like teardrops inside the rain

as I looked towards the sea

Francesca Bell's poems appear in many journals, including *B O D Y, ELLE, New Ohio Review, North American Review, Prairie Schooner, Rattle*, and *River Styx*. Her work has been nominated nine times for the Pushcart Prize, and she won the 2014 Neil Postman Award for Metaphor from *Rattle*. Her co-translations from Arabic appear in *Berkeley Poetry Review, Blue Lyra Review, Circumference, Four by Two*, and *Laghoo*. Her translations from German are forthcoming in *The Massachusetts Review*. She co-translated Shatha Abu Hnaish's book of poems, *A Love That Hovers Like a Bedeviling Mosquito* (Dar Fadaat, 2017), and Red Hen Press will publish her first collection, *Bright Stain*, in 2019.

John Bennett was born in Brooklyn, New York in 1938. He is the founder of Vagabond Press and the former editor of the small press magazine *Vagabond*. The magazine was started in 1966 and he published Charles Bukowski, Tom Kryss, d.a. levy, Ann Menebroker, William Wantling and many other poets, new or established. He also edited *Ragged Lion, A Tribute to Jack Micheline* as well as the Henry Miller tribute *Black Messiah*, both published by Vagabond Press. John Bennett has 39 published books to his credit– novels, short story collections, journalism, poetry and shards, a form of prose poem Bennett has made his own. He now lives in Ellensburg, Washington, where he writes, publishes and sends his shards out on a regular basis to a highly-appreciative and wide-spread email list.

Iris Berry is one of the true and original progenitors of the L.A. punk scene. Her lifetime spent in the City of Angels has resulted in over two decades worth of astonishing prose, poetry and music. Berry's writing has been widely anthologized in a number of journals and collections including *The Outlaw Bible of American Poetry*. *Two Blocks East of Vine*, her book of short stories, was published on Incommunicado Press. Berry's spoken word CDs "Life on the Edge in Stilettos" and "Collect Calls" received critical acclaim and allowed her fans to hear her writing in the way it was meant to be heard. She co-edited volume three of the best-selling *Underground Guide to Los Angeles* with long-time writing partner Pleasant Gehman and co-produced a series of burlesque and variety shows with comic and activist Margaret Cho called "The Sensuous Woman", all proceeds for charity. In 2012, Iris co-founded Punk Hostage Press with poet and long-time friend A. Razor.

Jane Blue has published three books of poetry and two chapbooks. The latest book is *Blood Moon* from FutureCycle Press, January 2014. Her poems have appeared in many journals, some well known, some very small presses, and more often now, on-line, which she likes because she has no more room in her bookcase and likes the reach of an on-line publication. She lives in California near the Sacramento River with her husband, Peter Rodman.

Laurel Ann Bogen is the author of 10 books of poetry and short fiction including *Washing a Language, Fission, The Last Girl in the Land of the Butterflies, The Burning, Do Iguanas Dance, Under the Moonlight?* and *Rag Tag We Kiss*. Her latest book, *Psychosis in the Produce Department: New and Selected Poems 1975-2015.* is published by Red Hen Press and includes QR codes that link to audio files of select poems in the collection.

William Seward Bonnie is a traveling artist who lives on the roads of America.

Rich Boucher resides in Albuquerque, New Mexico. Rich served two terms as a member of the Albuquerque Poet Laureate Program's Selection Committee, and also as a member of the 2008 & 2014 Albuquerque City Slam Teams. Rich's poems have appeared in *Gargoyle, Yellow Chair Review, The Nervous Breakdown, Apeiron Review, The Mas Tequila Review, Menacing Hedge, Lotus-eater, Cultural Weekly*, and *Tinderbox Poetry Journal*, among others, and he has work in the Write Bloody Publishing superhero anthology *MultiVerse*, which was released in the Fall of 2014.

MK Chavez writes poetry about real things, love, strippers, the beauty that can be found in ugliness, the mystery of feeling bad about feeling good, little birds, big consequences. Her work has been anthologized in both print and online literary journals. She plays an active role in the Bay Area literary scene. MK is one of the curators/hosts for the monthly reading series Lyrics & Dirges as well as co-organizer of The Berkeley Poetry Festival. She has been nominated for the Pushcart Prize and is the author of *Virgin Eyes* from Zeitgeist Press and *Next Exit #9* with John Sweet from Kendra Steiner Editions.

Sharon Coleman's a fifth-generation Northern Californian with a penchant for languages and their entangled word roots. She writes for *Poetry Flash*, co-curates the reading series Lyrics & Dirges and co-directs the Berkeley Poetry Festival. She's the author of a chapbook of poetry, *Half Circle* (Finishing Line), and a book of micro-fiction, *Paris Blinks* (Paper Press). Her most recent publications appear in *Your Impossible Voice, White Stag*, and *Ambush Review*. She's been nominated twice for a Pushcart and once for a micro award for blink fiction.

Paul Corman-Roberts is a core founder of the Beast Crawl Lit Fest. His most recent chap is *Notes From An Orgy* (Paper Press). He runs 2 regular reading series in Oakland CA and 739 irregular reading series throughout the Cosmos.

Dennis Cruz has been writing and performing poetry in los angeles for the last 25 years. His current collection of poetry: *MOTH WING TEA* was published by Punk Hostage Press in 2013. He lives in northeast los angeles with his wife and son.

Cassandra Dallett lives in Oakland, CA. Cassandra is a two-time Pushcart nominee and Literary Death Match winner. She has been published online and in many print magazines, such as *Slip Stream, Sparkle and Blink, Chiron Review, Stone Boat Review*, and *Great Weather for Media*. Cassandra reads often around the San Francisco Bay Area. Her first full-length book of poetry *Wet Reckless* (Manic D Press) was released in 2014. In 2015, she authored five chapbooks one of them, *On Sunday, A Finch* (Nomadic Press) was nominated for a California Book Award. Look for a new full-length collection *Collapse* from Nomadic Press in the fall of 2107.

Jessica Dawson is a modern-day Wendy. She is a contributing editor at Words Dance Publishing, Assistant Poetry Editor at *The Montucky Review* and has had her work published in various places (come on, you can Google it). She abhors self-promotion but requires an audience at all times, reads the dictionary for fun, speaks only in degrees of sarcasm and is more vulture than falcon, really.

Lisa Douglass is like a memory you wish you could remember sometimes and other times she is like a memory you wish you could forget. She has spent the last year making movies about witches who turn bad men into dolls. You can find more of her writing on her blog The Hurty is From all the Sin. She teaches writing in Los Angeles and makes her living as a photographer.

Alexis Rhone Fancher is the author of *How I Lost My Virginity to Michael Cohen and other heart stab poems*, (2014), *State of Grace: The Joshua Elegies*, (2015), and *Enter Here* (2017). She is published in *The Best American Poetry 2016, Rattle, Slipstream, Hobart, Cleaver, The MacGuffin, Poetry East, Plume, Tinderbox*, and elsewhere. Her photographs are published worldwide, including the cover of *Witness, Heyday*, and *Nerve Cowboy*, and a spread in *River Styx*. A multiple Pushcart Prize and Best of The Net nominee, Alexis is poetry editor of *Cultural Weekly*. She lives in Los Angeles. Find out more at: www.alexisrhonefancher.com

Bill Gainer, the legendary Northern California writer, known for the openness of his confessional poetry, has contributed to the literary scene as an award winning writer, editor, promoter, publicist and poet – he currently edits for the Pen Award winning R.L. Crow Publications. Gainer has a long standing love of the short poem, but finds himself often more recognized for his longer pieces. He continues to read and work with a wide range of poets and writers – from the emerging to the renowned. Gainer is nationally published and remains a sought after reader. He is a past winner of the S.F. Beat Museum's Poetry Contest and a recent winner of the Sacramento News and Review's Flash Fiction Contest. His latest book is *The Fine Art of Poisoning*. Visit him at billgainer.com.

S.A. Griffin lives, loves and works in Los Angeles.

Jason Hardung's work has appeared in many journals and magazines including: *Monkey Bicycle, Evergreen Review, Metazen, Entropy, The Common, Thought Catalog, Word Riot, Thrasher Magazine, Heavy Feather Review* and *The New York Quarterly*. He has two books of poetry out on Epic Rites Press and Lummox Press. He has been an editor for Wolverine Farm Publishing and the *Front Range Review* in Fort Collins, Colorado where he lives in a commune. In 2013 he was Poet Laureate of Fort Collins.

Dustin Holland lives with his friends in Longmont, Colorado and helps organize a poetry reading/art show/concert series called "Don't Yell At Me" (www.facebook.com/donotyellatme)(https://instagram.com/dontyellat.me/)

Ellaraine Lockie is a widely published and awarded poet, nonfiction book author and essayist. Her thirteenth chapbook, *Tripping with the Top Down*, was just released from FootHills Publishing. Earlier collections have won the Encircle Publications Chapbook Contest, Poetry Forum's Chapbook Contest Prize, San Gabriel Valley Poetry Festival Chapbook Contest, the Aurorean's Chapbook Choice Award and Best Individual Collection Award from *Purple Patch Magazine* in England. Ellaraine teaches poetry workshops and serves as Poetry Editor for the lifestyles magazine, *Lilipoh*.

John Macker lives and writes in Santa Fe, New Mexico. He was contributing editor to the *Desert Shovel Review* and Albuquerque's *Malpais Review*. He has published 5 full length books of poetry. His most recent work can be found in Denver woodblock artist Leon Loughridge's 8 volume folio set of prints and poems entitled "Gorge Songs."

Ellyn Maybe, Southern California based poet, United States Artist nominee 2012, has performed both nationally and internationally as a solo artist and with her band. Her work has been included in many anthologies and she is the author of numerous books. She also has a critically acclaimed poetry/music album, *Rodeo for the Sheepish*. In addition to her band, her latest poetry/music project is called Ellyn and Robbie. Please visit ellynmaybe.com and ellynandrobbie.com for more.

Ann Menebroker, a poet of international stature and a Sacramento resident, wrote more than 20 books of poetry and appeared in numerous anthologies including *The Outlaw Bible of American Poetry*. Ann curated a poetry journal and contributed to a wide range of small press poetry magazines. Early in her career, she co-edited *Landing Signals,* the first anthology of works by Sacramento poets. Ann passed away at the age of 80 in 2016. She is remembered fondly.

Sheila E. Murphy is an American text and visual poet who has been writing and publishing actively since 1978. Her most recent 2 books are collaborative visual poetry, with K.S. Ernst and John M. Bennett. Murphy is a prolific writer and has authored numerous titles in poetry. She is also a visual artist, organizational consultant, and teacher who has lived all of her adult life in Phoenix.

Alexandra Naughton is Editor-in-Chief of Be About It Press. Her first novel, *American Mary*, was published by Civil Coping Mechanisms in 2016.

s. Nicholas lives and teaches in the San Bernardino mountains of Southern California. She has a degree in English/World Literature and Psychology from Pitzer College, a Master's in Education from Claremont Graduate University, and an MFA in Creative Writing from Cal State San Bernardino. Her first chapbook, *apology for my distractedness* was recently published by Islands for Writers Press. For further reading dates, as well as vegetarian recipes, please visit her website www.sNicholas.net or follow her on Twitter @ shalisorange.

A. Razor began writing and publishing around 1980 in various underground zines and publications, first in the Los Angeles area, then ever expanding outward from there as he was discovered by Drew Blood Press, Ltd. in 1984, where he published 11 chapbooks up to 1995. He has read his work at many readings and spoken word events over the years and been published in many types of publications. He became a member of the Hollywood Institute of Poetics in Los Angeles, CA in 2009. He has participated recently in the Poets In Prison panel at Beyond Baroque and the 2011 ALOUD reading series held at the Downtown Los Angeles Public Library. In 2012 he teamed up with Iris Berry to launch Punk Hostage Press. His long anticipated offering, *Better Than A Gun In A Knife Fight* was released in May, 2012 on Punk Hostage Press, edited by Iris Berry with an introduction by Bucky Sinister. Other books include *Drawn Blood: Collected Works on D.B.P.,Ltd. 1985-1995, Small Catastrophes in a Big World, Beaten Up Beaten Down, Half-Century Status.*

Luivette Resto was born in Aguas Buenas, Puerto Rico and raised in the Bronx. The first in her family to graduate from college, Resto earned a BA at Cornell University and an MFA at the University of Massachusetts at Amherst, where she studied with Martín Espada. Resto is the author of the poetry collections *Unfinished Portrait* (2008), which was a finalist for the Paterson Poetry Prize, and *Ascension* (2013). A CantoMundo Fellow, she has taught at Citrus College and Mt. San Antonio College, and has served as a contributing editor for *Kweli Journal.* She lives with her family in the Los Angeles area, and hosts the monthly reading series La Palabra in Highland Park.

Kevin Ridgeway lives and writes in Long Beach, California. His work has been published in several small press and underground literary journals, zines and anthologies from across the globe. Recent poems can be found in *Chiron Review, Nerve Cowboy, BIG HAMMER, San Pedro River Review, Misfit Magazine, Right Hand Pointing, Bicycle Review, Cultural Weekly* and *The Mas Tequila Review*, among others. He has been nominated for the Pushcart Prize and Best of the Net. He is the author of six chapbooks of poetry, including *All the Rage* (Electric Windmill Press, 2013), *On the Burning Shore* (Arroyo Seco Press, 2014) and *Contents Under Pressure* (Crisis Chronicles Press, 2015).

Ryan Snellman: Haunting the ghosted streets of Ballard looking for meaning in between the raindrops.

William Taylor Jr. lives and writes in the Tenderloin neighborhood of San Francisco. His work has been published widely in journals across the globe, including *The New York Quarterly, The Chiron Review*, and *Catamaran Literary Reader.* He is the author of numerous books of poetry, and a collection of short fiction. He is a Pushcart Prize nominee and was a recipient of the 2013 Kathy Acker Award. *To Break the Heart of the Sun* is his latest collection of poetry. He recently edited *Cockymoon: Selected Poems of Jack Micheline*, published by Zeitgeist Press in 2017.

Michael N. Thompson likes bacon, fantasy football and *Twin Peaks.* His poetry has appeared in numerous literary journals including *Word Riot, Toronto Quarterly* and *San Pedro River*

Review. He is the author of four poetry collections. Michael is currently at work on his first novel, *Postcards From An Assassin*. www.michaelnthompson.com

Richard Vargas was born in Compton, CA, attended schools in Compton, Lynwood, and Paramount. He earned his B.A. at Cal State University, Long Beach, where he studied under Gerald Locklin and Richard Lee. He edited/published five issues of *The Tequila Review*, 1978-1980. His first book, *McLife*, was featured on *Garrison Keillor's Writer's Almanac*, in February, 2006. A second book, *American Jesus*, was published by Tia Chucha Press, 2007. His third book, *Guernica, revisited,* was published April 2014, by Press 53. (Once again, a poem from the book was featured on *Writer's Almanac* to kick off National Poetry Month.) Vargas received his MFA from the University of New Mexico, 2010. He was recipient of the 2011 Taos Summer Writers' Conference's Hispanic Writer Award, and was on the faculty of the 2012 10th National Latino Writers Conference. Currently, he resides in Rockford, IL, where he edits/publishes *The Más Tequila Review*. www.richardvargaspoet.com

Scott Wannberg was a human's human and a poet's poet. Born in Venice, California February 1953, Scott spent the last three years of his life in Florence, Oregon where he left the party too soon at the age of 58 in August 2011. His most recent book *The Official Language of Yes* was published by Perceval Press in 2015.